GRAYSON

VITAL STATS

Full Name: Richard "Dick" Grayson

Occupation: Agent of Spyral, gymnastics teacher

Height: 5ft 10in

Weight: 175 lbs

Base: Saint Hadrian's Finishing School for Girls, England

Allies: Batman, the Batman Family, Helena Bertinelli, Starfire

Foes: The Joker, Prankster, Paragon, Tony Zucco

POWERS AND ABILITIES

Highly skilled acrobat; natural athlete; martial artist; extremely intelligent; trained by Batman; can alter appearance via identity protection implants.

LIGHTS OUT AT MIDNIGHT

Grayson's adventures with Spyral have put him in direct opposition with the vigilante known as the Midnighter on several occasions. What Midnighter doesn't know is that Grayson is secretly a double agent for Batman.

Equipped with mind-influencing "hypnos"

Favorite weapons are escrima sticks

Belt equipped with variety of hi-tech gadgets

Soon after young trapeze artist Dick Grayson watched his parents fall to their deaths, he embarked on a new chapter in his life as Bruce Wayne's adopted son and Batman's partner, Robin. After growing into a Super Hero in his own right—Nightwing—Dick later retired that name after a near-death experience, and went to work at the spy agency Spyral as Agent 37.

"We've got some lives to save."

RED HOOD

VITAL STATS

Real Name: Jason Todd

Occupation: Vigilante for hire

Height: 6ft

Weight: 180 lbs

Base: Los Angeles, California

Allies: The Outlaws, the Batman Family, Talia al Ghūl, the League of Assassins

Foes: The Joker, Rā's al Ghūl, the Untitled

POWERS AND ABILITIES

Martial artist; skilled detective and gymnast; adept assassin; impressive intellect; trained by Batman; armored suit equipped with offensive and defensive devices.

OUTLAW BY CHOICE

Jason Todd was given a second lease on life thanks to Talia al Ghūl and the healing properties of the Lazarus Pit. He transitioned from Robin to the Red Hood, and teamed up with other like-minded heroes.

Jason Todd was discovered by the Joker at an early age. The Joker had Jason's father arrested and faked his mother's death, maneuvering the boy into position to become Batman's newest Robin. Now in a position to destabilize the Batman family, the Joker killed Jason, not knowing that the young man would later return to life as the Red Hood.

"I don't work for just anyone."

Wears hi-tech protective helmet

Armored suit equipped with myriad devices

Red bat symbol on his costume

RED ROBIN

HERO

VITAL STATS

Real Name: Timothy Drake

Occupation: Hero

Height: 5ft 6in

Weight: 131 lbs

Base: New York City

Allies: The Teen Titans, Batman, the Batman Family, Spoiler

Foes: The Penguin, the Mad Hatter, the Joker

POWERS AND ABILITIES

Martial artist; skilled detective and gymnast; impressive intellect; excellent computer hacker; protective glider suit equipped with myriad offensive and defensive devices; natural born leader.

A DIFFERENT DRUMMER
As the third person to bear the name Robin, Tim Drake decided to set himself apart from the crowd and opted for the title Red Robin instead. After serving as Batman's partner for a time, he soon formed his own team, the Teen Titans.

Red Robin's role as the leader of the Teen Titans has placed him in many life-and-death situations, including facing the villain known as Grymm.

A gifted gymnast and scholar, high school student Tim Drake wanted nothing more than to fight crime with the Dark Knight. To that end, he used his computer hacking skills to steal the Penguin's fortune. The Penguin retaliated against Tim's family, forcing Batman to place them in protective custody. Tim stayed in Gotham City and became Batman's partner, Red Robin.

"I want to apply for the job."

BATGIRL

VITAL STATS

Real Name: Barbara Gordon

Occupation: Hero, graduate student

Height: 5ft 11in

Weight: 135 lbs

Base: Burnside, Gotham City

Allies: The Birds of Prey, the Batman Family, James Gordon

Foes: The Joker, James Gordon, Jr., Knightfall, Velvet Tiger

POWERS AND ABILITIES

Expert martial artist and gymnast; intelligent and excellent strategist; natural leader; athletic and agile; uses compactible Batcycle; trained by Batman.

PACKING A PUNCH

Batgirl has worn several costumes over the years. She adopted her second official uniform when returning to crime fighting after a temporary hiatus. This costume was highly armored and utilized all of Batman's technology.

The daughter of police commissioner James Gordon, Barbara Gordon idolized Batman from a young age. One day, at police headquarters, Barbara adopted a police-developed Batsuit to protect her brother from an escaping criminal. After Batman complimented her on her actions, she realized her true calling and donned a mask and cape as Batgirl.

"Shut up and hug, tough girl."

Can remember with expert precision

Designed her own protective costume

Smartphone to use social media to her advantage

Fully stocked Utility Belt

LADY BLACKHAWK

HERO

VITAL STATS

Real Name: Zinda Blake

Occupation: Hero, pilot

Height: 5ft 7in

Weight: 117 lbs

Base: Mobile

Allies: The Birds of Prey, Blackhawks

Foes: The Penguin, Killer Shark

POWERS AND ABILITIES

Expert pilot, who can handle any kind of aircraft with ease; adept hand-to-hand combatant; proficient marksman.

BLACKHAWK DOWN

Zinda Blake has never been one to back down from a challenge, and more often than not can be found brawling in whatever bar she's chosen to drink in on any particular night. Nevertheless, she became a valued ally to the Birds of Prey.

Sign up at recruitment center ear you.

Lady Blackhawk was a member of the Blackhawks, a secretive squadron of ace pilots who fought during World War II. After traveling through time, Lady Blackhawk temporarily served as a pilot for the Birds of Prey. More unruly than her fellow Super Heroes, Lady Blackhawk has nevertheless proven that she can hold her own in nearly any fight.

Pilot jacket is flexible to allow ease of movement

Old fashioned costume shows difficulty adjusting to modern times

Wears traditional Blackhawk symbol

"Gonna be one beautiful flight."

STRIX

VITAL STATS

Real Name: Mary Turner

Occupation: Hero, former assassin

Height: 5ft 7in

Weight: 120 lbs

Base: Gotham City

Allies: Batgirl, the Birds of Prey, Talon, the Secret Six

Foes: The Court of Owls, Mr. Freeze, Rās al Ghūl

POWERS AND ABILITIES

Expert assassin and fighter trained by the Court of Owls; natural acrobat; genius IQ; extremely observant; possesses healing factor and can "die" and be brought back to life again.

ROUGH START

After encountering Batgirl during a battle against the Court of Owls, Strix was recruited to join the Birds of Prey. There was some friction between the teammates at first, but she soon became a trusted member of their entourage.

During an attack on the United States by Japan in 1944, a girl named Mary was badly scarred, losing her tongue as well as her family. She found work at Haly's Circus, but despite being a talented aerialist, she stayed behind the scenes as her face frightened audiences. She was recruited by the Court of Owls, but broke free of their influence thanks to Batgirl.

"Hrrrnnn!"

Altered costume slightly to fool the Court of Owls

Does not speak, just grunts

Clawed fingertips on gloves

EL GAUCHO

VITAL STATS

Real Name: Santiago Vargas

Occupation: Hero, wealthy socialite

Height: 6ft 1in

Weight: 215 lbs

Base: Buenos Aires, Argentina

Allies: Batman, Batman, Inc., the Club of Heroes

Foes: The Club of Villains, Leviathan, Dr. Hurt, Scorpiana, El Sombrero

POWERS AND ABILITIES

Highly trained hand-to-hand combatant; usually drives motorcycle during missions; intelligent and extremely wealthy.

THE MARK OF GAUCHO

El Gaucho and Batman once teamed up to track down Dr. Dedalus, a Spyral agent. The Dark Knight's respect for El Gaucho is perhaps due to him seeing a bit of his childhood hero, Zorro, in the crime fighter.

In the early days of Batman's career, billionaire John Mayhew recruited him to be part of the Club of Heroes alongside other international crime fighters. While Batman didn't find the Club to his liking, he later enlisted many of its members into his own team, Batman, Inc., including El Gaucho, who represented his native country, Argentina.

"...the tango of death is over!"

El Gaucho was secretly Agent 33 for Spyral. However, he turned on his boss, Dr. Dedalus, and saved Batman's life.

THE KNIGHT

HERO

VITAL STATS

Real Name: Cyril Sheldrake

Occupation: Hero

Height: 6ft 2in

Weight: 209 lbs

Base: Wordenshire, England

Allies: The Squire, the Knight I, Batman, Batman, Inc., the Club of Heroes

Foes: Springheeled Jack, Morris Men, Leviathan, Heretic

POWERS AND ABILITIES

Expert martial artist; skilled detective and gymnast; impressive intellect; armored suit equipped with myriad devices; natural born leader; vast supply of vehicles and weapons.

KNIGHT IN WAITING

The Knight and his partner, the Squire, were fairly inseparable, often spending time at their favorite pub, the Time in a Bottle. When the Knight was killed, the Squire took his place after mourning her old friend.

Cyril Sheldrake used to be known as the Squire—a loyal sidekick to his father Percy, the original Knight. The pair were the so-called Batman and Robin of England. As the Squire, he joined the Club of Heroes with his father. Later graduating to the position of the Knight, Cyril would become a member of Batman, Inc., and perish in a deadly battle with the Heretic.

"Don't let them win, Beryl..."

Being the Knight was a family tradition, which Cyril took on gladly. He stepped into his father's large shoes, and made the role of the Knight his own.

THE HOOD

VITAL STATS

Real Name: George Cross
Occupation: Hero, spy
Height: 5ft 10in
Weight: 172 lbs
Base: London, England
Allies: Batman, Batman, Inc., Spyral, T.H.E.Y.
Foes: Leviathan, Dr. Dedalus

POWERS AND ABILITIES

Highly trained hand-to-hand combatant and martial artist; athletic and agile; expert spy; access to Batman, Inc. equipment as well as his own Hood-themed jet; fully stocked Utility Belt; excellent detective skills.

PICK A SIDE

The Hood kept his involvement in the clandestine organization known as Spyral a secret from his Batman, Inc. cohorts. However, the Hood was fighting on Batman's side all along, especially when it came to his opposition of Leviathan.

Inspired by Robin Hood, George Cross takes money from criminals and gives it to the poor. When Batman first met the Hood in London, he was impressed, and he thought of the British hero when he later formed Batman, Inc. The Hood accepted the Dark Knight's offer to join the organization, and used the opportunity to become a triple agent, working for England's Super Secret Service (T.H.E.Y.) and Spyral.

Styles himself after Robin Hood

Costume based on medieval knight armor

Cross logo hints at his real name

"World's greatest assassins... meet Batman's front line."

DARK RANGER

VITAL STATS

Real Name: Johnny Riley
Occupation: Hero
Height: 5ft 10in
Weight: 181 lbs
Base: Melbourne, Australia
Allies: Batman, Inc.,
Dark Ranger I, Batman,
the Squire
Foes: Leviathan,
La Muerte en Vida

POWERS AND ABILITIES

Utilizes armored suit
inherited from the
original Dark Ranger; jet
pack enables flight; carries
pistol that fires electro-stun
blasts; uniform has pouches
that contain various hi-tech
gadgets and weapons.

PEP TALK

Dark Ranger was sworn into Batman,
Inc. by Batman himself. Always a bit
cynical, Riley was convinced to give
Batman, Inc. a try by the Squire,
and the two even became
romantically involved.

Johnny Riley used to be the Super
Hero sidekick to the Ranger—the
Australian version of Batman. As the
years passed, the Ranger became the
Dark Ranger and Scout gave up the
heroic life. However, when the Dark
Ranger was murdered, Riley donned
his mentor's suit and took up the
mantle of the Dark Ranger. He was
soon recruited into Batman, Inc.

*"You gotta let me try out
one of your batarangs."*

The original Ranger traded in a boy scout look for
riot gear. The second Dark Ranger, Johnny Riley,
follows suit, carrying an array of non-lethal weapons.

BAT-COW

ALLY

VITAL STATS

Full Name: Bat-Cow

Occupation: Robin's pet

Height: 5ft

Weight: 1,252 lbs

Base: Gotham City

Allies: Robin, Alfred Pennyworth, the Batman Family

Foes: Meat eaters

POWERS AND ABILITIES

Average female Guernsey cow.

BAT-ZOO

While the pets in the Batcave are supposed to belong to Robin, Alfred Pennyworth seems to take on the lion's share of the work when it comes to feeding and caring for Bat-Cow, whether he's happy about it or not.

Robin and Batman were fighting villains in a slaughterhouse, when they realized it was an ambush. An assassin named Goatboy had tried and failed to destroy Robin. Taking pity on the last remaining cow, Robin declared himself a vegetarian and took the animal home with him. With mask-like coloring on his face and a star brand on his rump, Bat-Cow became Robin's newest pet.

After Robin was killed by the villain Heretic, then brought back to life, he returned to the Batcave, happy that Alfred had taken care of his pets.

"Moo!"

THOMAS WAYNE

VITAL STATS

Full Name: Thomas Wayne

Occupation: Surgeon, philanthropist

Height: 6ft 2in

Weight: 210 lbs

Base: Gotham City

Allies: Martha and Bruce Wayne, Alfred and Jarvis Pennyworth, Lucius Fox

Foes: Joe Chill, the Court of Owls

POWERS AND ABILITIES

Highly skilled surgeon; powerful connections in the business world; amateur mechanic and inventor; extremely intelligent and loving father.

THE LAST NIGHT

Thomas and Martha Wayne's fate was sealed the night they took their son to a screening of The Mark of Zorro in Gotham City. After the film, they were shot dead by Joe Chill during a botched robbery.

Thomas Wayne was a loving husband and father. Born into a wealthy family, Thomas created quite a career for himself as a surgeon. Though he was killed when his son Bruce was just a boy, he had nevertheless created many memories with his son, including showing Bruce a Witch's Eye, a hi-tech visual mapping device that later helped inspire the creation of the Batman.

"What do you love about Gotham, Bruce?"

Hat bears logo similar to Robin's

Wears casual attire in spare time when tinkering with mechanics

Doted on his son, often giving gifts

MARTHA WAYNE

ALLY

VITAL STATS

Full Name: Martha Wayne

Occupation: Mother, philanthropist

Height: 5ft 4in

Weight: 108 lbs

Base: Gotham City

Allies: Thomas and Bruce Wayne, Alfred and Jarvis Pennyworth

Foes: Joe Chill, the Court of Owls

POWERS AND ABILITIES

Empathetic philanthropist; powerful contacts in Gotham City's most elite social circles, partially due to Kane family name (Martha's maiden name); intelligent and giving mother.

MOTHER OF INNOVATION

Martha Wayne, a civic-minded woman, was upset at the state of Gotham City's education system. To fix the problem, she created a new school for Gotham City's underprivileged, despite receiving threats from the mayor's office.

A loving mother to Bruce Wayne, Martha Wayne was a philanthropist who stood up to Gotham City's corrupt mayor's office, not knowing it was backed by the violent, secret organization, the Court of Owls. The Court of Owls caused Martha to have a car "accident." and her loyal butler Jarvis Pennyworth was killed by a Talon assassin as well.

> *"You're the bravest boy in Gotham, Bruce."*

While her life was full of tragedy, and would soon end thanks to Joe Chill, Martha spent much of her short life doting on her son, Bruce.

JAMES GORDON

VITAL STATS

Full Name: James W. Gordon

Occupation: Deputized vigilante, former police commissioner

Height: 5ft 9in

Weight: 168 lbs

Base: Gotham City

Allies: Batman, the Batman Family, Batgirl, G.C.P.D.

Foes: The Joker, Mr. Bloom, James Gordon, Jr.

POWERS AND ABILITIES

Extremely physically fit; natural leader; expertise in police procedure; former marine; robotic suit armed with crime-fighting equipment.

BATMAN 2.0

After the real Batman seemingly died, James Gordon stepped up to fill the role as a fully deputized agent of the law. Wearing a Batsuit inside a giant bat-themed robot suit, the 46-year-old does his best to fill Batman's shoes.

James Gordon worked his way up the chain of command at the Gotham City Police Department, fighting corruption at every turn. He eventually became commissioner, but was framed for murder and incarcerated. Gordon's job was not waiting for him when he was exonerated. However, he accepted an offer from Geri Powers to become the G.C.P.D.'s official Batman instead.

"Sometimes, you just have to get out and walk the beat."

Haircut harks back to his days as a Marine

Shaved mustache to resemble Batman

Highly trained fighter

Got back in shape to become Batman

GERI POWERS

ALLY

VITAL STATS

Full Name: Geri Powers

Occupation: CEO of Powers International

Height: 5ft 5in

Weight: 119 lbs

Base: Gotham City

Allies: .G.C.P.D, James Gordon

Foe: Mayor Sebastian Hady

POWERS AND ABILITIES

CEO of one of the most powerful businesses in Gotham City and the world; oversees the technology for G.C.P.D.'s Batman project; powerful police and business connections; highly intelligent and motivated.

THE POWER BEHIND THE BATMAN

Geri Powers oversaw the creation and implementation of the robotic armored Batsuit that James Gordon pilots in conjunction with the Gotham City Police Department. She helps Gordon get used to his new role and is his biggest supporter.

Powers International has been one of the most important corporations in Gotham City for centuries. After Wayne Enterprises was made defunct during a scheme launched by Lincoln March and the Cluemaster, Powers acquired the company and its assets. CEO Geri Powers gave the G.C.P.D. the technology to create a Batman of its own when the real Batman was presumed dead.

Gordon agreed to adopt the mantle of Batman after Powers pointed out that none of the G.C.P.D.'s recruits would be the "right" Batman.

"Are you ready to be Batman...
Commissioner Gordon?"

PHILIP KANE

VITAL STATS

Full Name: Philip Kane

Occupation: Former Wayne Enterprises CEO

Height: 5ft 11in

Weight: 184 lbs

Base: Gotham City

Allies: The Riddler, Bruce Wayne, Martha Wayne

Foes: The Red Hood Gang

POWERS AND ABILITIES

Access to Wayne Enterprises funds and technology; criminal ties to the Red Hood Gang; held powerful business connections; gifted eye for business; advised by Edward Nygma.

KANE AND ABLE

The brother of Bruce Wayne's mother, Martha Wayne, Philip Kane had been trying to track Bruce down for years. Kane eventually located Bruce at his base, a townhouse near Crime Alley, the street where the Waynes were killed.

When Thomas and Martha Wayne were murdered and their son Bruce left to travel the world, Philip Kane was put in charge of the family business and merged Kane Chemical and Wayne Industries. On Bruce's return to Gotham City, he found out his uncle was working with the Red Hood Gang. After Kane's death at the hands of Red Hood One, Bruce reclaimed his company.

"I never meant for things to turn out this way."

On the night Batman foiled the Red Hood Gang's raid of A.C.E. Chemical, Philip Kane was killed by Red Hood One after trying to save Batman.

VICKI VALE

VITAL STATS

Full Name: Vicki Vale

Occupation: Journalist for the *Gotham Gazette*

Height: 5ft 8in

Weight: 115 lbs

Base: Gotham City

Allies: Bruce Wayne, Jason Bard, Warren Stacey

Foes: The Penguin, Carmine Falcone

POWERS AND ABILITIES

Ace reporter with a knack for finding major news stories; extremely intelligent and a detective in her own right; athletic and capable of self-defense against attackers.

HANDS ON

Unafraid to get her hands dirty while on the hunt for a scoop, Vicki once lashed out at a would-be mugger, holding a taser to his face in order to get information from the hardened criminal.

Vicki Vale is one of the *Gotham Gazette*'s most respected reporters. While she's usually particular about her sources and their credibility, she was once manipulated by former police lieutenant Jason Bard to cast him as a hero in the eyes of Gotham City's public. While her articles landed her a promotion, it took a lot of apologizing from Bard to win back her trust.

"It's insane...but not impossible."

Vicki Vale has several ethical coworkers at the *Gotham Gazette*, including crime editor Warren Stacey.

MAYOR SEBASTIAN HADY

ROGUE

VITAL STATS

Full Name: Sebastian Hady
Occupation: Mayor of Gotham City
Height: 5ft 6in
Weight: 202 lbs
Base: Gotham City
Allies: G.C.P.D., the Penguin, Carmine Falcone
Foes: James Gordon, Batman, Batman, Inc.

POWERS AND ABILITIES

Wealthy connections; control over Gotham City's police department; persuasive and influential networker.

MONEY ON HIS MIND

With a mind for money, Mayor Hady is quick to act in his own selfish interests. He once made a deal with Caldwell Technologies, not realizing their CEO was a super-villain known as Wrath.

Gotham City is a corrupt metropolis, so it only follows that its leader, Mayor Sebastian Hady, is an unethical and unapologetic individual. Hady originally ran for mayor in the year Batman first began to operate in Gotham City. These days, Hady doesn't shy away from working hand in hand with organized criminals, including the Penguin.

Puts on a phony demeanor to appear likeable

Has gained weight since his campaign years

Well-dressed to look the part

"Batman is no longer welcome in Gotham City."

GOTHAM ACADEMY FACULTY

VITAL STATS

Faculty includes:

Headmaster
"Hammerhead" Hammer,

Professor Isla MacPherson,

Professor Hugo Strange,

Dr. Kirk Langstrom,

Coach Humphreys,

Mr. Scarlett,

"Aunt" Harriet,

Mr. Trent,

Professor Achilles Milo
(former teacher)

THE CUSTODIAN

Gotham Academy is steeped in legends, one of which is the story of the Custodian, a mysterious hero who stalks the campus grounds, fighting off threats. In reality, the Custodian is really Headmaster Hammer protecting his students.

Professor Isla MacPherson

Gotham Academy is a prestigious boarding school that has attracted expert teachers from many different walks of life. There are science classes taught by the Man-Bat, Dr. Kirk Langstrom, and Professor Milo. Another Professor, Hugo Strange, serves as the school's counselor and there's "Bookworm" Mr. Scarlett, as well as kindly "Aunt" Harriet.

"Welcome to Gotham Academy."

Mr. Scarlett, the school "Bookworm"

Headmaster "Hammerhead" Hammer

HALY'S CIRCUS

VITAL STATS

Group Name:
Haly's Circus

Base: Mobile

Allies: Dick
Grayson, the
Court of Owls

Foes: Tony Zucco,
the Joker

**Notable Former
Members:**
C.C. Haly,
Dick Grayson,
John Grayson, Mary
Grayson, Bryan Haly,
Raya Vestri, Talon (Calvin
Rose), Talon (William
Cobb), Strix, Saiko

GOTHAM CITY NO MORE
For years, Haly's Circus
made Gotham City a
staple on its tour route.
However, when two
members of its star
act, the Flying Graysons,
were killed by gangster
Tony Zucco, the circus
didn't return to the city
for almost five years.

From all appearances, Haly's Circus
seems like an innocent institution, a
touring group of performers with an
extensive history. But most customers
are unaware of the dark secret that
lurks beneath the surface. Decades
ago, the nefarious Court of Owls
made a deal with Haly's to recruit the
circus's best and brightest stars to
serve as the Court's Talon assassins.

*"Ladies and gentlemen...the star
of Haly's Circus...Dick Grayson!"*

A star member of the Flying Graysons trapeze
act, Dick was a prime target for the Court of
Owls, but he managed to escape life as a Talon.

HOLLY ROBINSON

VITAL STATS

Full Name: Holly Robinson
Occupation: Former Hero
Height: 5ft 3½in
Weight: 115 lbs
Base: Mobile
Allies: Catwoman, Slam Bradley, Harley Quinn
Foes: Black Mask, Film Freak

POWERS AND ABILITIES

Extremely fit and agile; adept hand-to-hand combatant with an emphasis on boxing techniques; proficient in the use of Catwoman's equipment.

CATWOMAN IN TRAINING

Holly Robinson feels a true love for Gotham City's East End, and felt the need to protect it during Catwoman's brief retirement. Unfortunately, she never quite settled into the demanding role.

Holly Robinson grew up in a troubled home, and eventually ran away to try living on her own in Gotham City's East End. With a rough road ahead of her, Holly was fortunate enough to befriend Selina Kyle, and learned of Selina's fledgling career as the cat burglar Catwoman. Holly even briefly donned the Catwoman costume herself when Selina temporarily retired.

Quick-witted and fast to react to danger

Slight build enables stealth

Thin frame from her life living on the streets

"Gee, it truly is a glamorous profession!"

THE JUSTICE LEAGUE

VITAL STATS

Team Name: The Justice League

Base: Watchtower satellite in Earth's orbit

Allies: Black Lightning, the Teen Titans, Black Canary

Foes: Darkseid, Anti-Monitor, the Crime Syndicate

Members:
Batman, Superman, Wonder Woman, Aquaman, Green Lantern (Hal Jordan), the Flash, Cyborg, Shazam, Power Ring, Martian Manhunter (former), Firestorm (former), Element Woman (former), Atomica (traitor), Lex Luthor, Captain Cold

NEW PARTNERSHIPS
It took some time for the founding Justice League members to trust one another. Some members, like Batman and Superman, began working together as partners outside of their Justice League missions.

The Justice League first formed when the other-dimensional tyrant Darkseid attempted to conquer Earth. Batman, Wonder Woman, Superman, Green Lantern, Cyborg, Aquaman, and the Flash successfully fought back, and decided to team up to battle other large-scale threats. Their roster has changed a few times, but they remain unwavering in their mission.

"You can call us... the Super Seven!"

The Justice League inducted "reformed" villains, Lex Luthor and Captain Cold, into their ranks after Luthor helped defeat the Crime Syndicate.

SUPERGIRL

HERO

VITAL STATS

Real Name: Kara Zor-El
Occupation: Hero
Height: 5ft 5in
Weight: 120 lbs
Base: Mobile
Allies: Superman, Superboy, the Justice League United, Steel
Foes: Jochi, Silver Banshee, H'el

POWERS AND ABILITIES

Super-strength; super-speed; superhuman reflexes, durability, senses, and endurance; flight; heat vision; freeze breath; X-ray vision; access to advanced Kryptonian technology; powers derived from Earth's yellow sun.

WORLD'S FINEST

In order to defeat the threat of the alien Jochi, Superman and Batman had to pick two champion allies to compete in Warworld's deadly gladiatorial arena. Superman chose Steel and Supergirl and Batman chose Red Hood and Batgirl.

Like Clark Kent, she has freeze breath

Wears the El family S-Shield

Can fly at high speeds

Kara Zor-El came from a prestigious family who lived in Argo City, one of the biggest metropolises on planet Krypton. Her scientist father, Zor-El, was Jor-El's brother. As Jor-El built a rocket ship to allow his baby Kal-El to escape Krypton's destruction, Zor-El created an escape pod for his daughter. Kara found her way to Earth and adopted the guise of Supergirl.

"You have to trust me to find my own way."

WONDER WOMAN

VITAL STATS

Real Name: Diana

Occupation: Hero, queen, God of War

Height: 6ft

Weight: 165 lbs

Base: Themyscira

Allies: Superman, Orion, the Justice League

Foes: Cheetah, Circe, the First Born

POWERS AND ABILITIES

Godly blood grants her super-strength, endurance, and agility; power of flight; Bracelets of Victory can deflect bullets; expert fighter and strategist; Lasso of Truth forces others to tell the truth; extremely wise and empathetic.

HEAR HER ROAR

Wonder Woman has occasionally changed her armor, but always retains the "star" iconography that represents her family lineage. An emissary of peace, she is also a true warrior at heart.

Diana is the daughter of the god Zeus and Hippolyta, the ruler of Themyscira, an island of female warriors called the Amazons. Diana grew up a princess completely isolated from the rest of the world. When a pilot named Steve Trevor crashed on Themyscira, Diana learned of the outside world and soon traveled there as her people's representative and a true Super Hero—Wonder Woman.

"It's a big, strange, and wondrous universe."

Armor forged by god Hephaestus

Tiara a sign of regal lineage

Bracelets of Victory can produce blades

Flexible armor for ease of movement

Lasso can be used to attack or defend

AQUAMAN

VITAL STATS

Real Name:
Arthur Curry

Occupation: Hero, king
of Atlantis

Height: 6ft 1in

Weight: 325 lbs

Base: Atlantis

Allies: Mera, the Justice
League, the Others

Foes: Black Manta, Ocean
Master, the Trench

POWERS AND ABILITIES
Can breathe underwater;
can communicate with and
control sea life; ruler of
underwater kingdom of
Atlantis; super-strength;
trained fighter and natural
leader; swims incredibly fast.

FISH OUT OF WATER
Batman and Aquaman have fought
side-by-side on many missions as part
of the Justice League. The two have
also teamed up as partners on occasion,
including the time they battled Rās al
Ghūl on a remote island in the Pacific.

Arthur Curry was born to a
lighthouse keeper and an Atlantean
queen, and raised on land when his
mother returned to the sea. Thanks
to his ability to breathe underwater
and communicate with sea life, Arthur
became known as Aquaman when he
was a young man. The rightful king of
Atlantis, he uses his abilities to fight
for creatures on land and in the ocean.

Body can bear
pressures of
the deep

Blond hair rare
in Atlantis

Wears
scale-like
uniform

Carries
trident to
use as
weapon

*"So who's in charge here?
I vote me."*

GREEN LANTERN

VITAL STATS

Real Name: Harold (Hal) Jordan
Occupation: Hero
Height: 6ft 2in
Weight: 186 lbs
Base: Mobile, Coast City
Allies: The Justice League, Green Lantern Corps
Foes: Sinestro, Red Lanterns, Black Hand

POWERS AND ABILITIES

Expert pilot; natural leader; Green Lantern ring can create physical manifestations of anything its user imagines; it also allows for flight, force fields, and space travel, and can impart encyclopedic knowledge to its wearer.

EMERALD KNIGHT
Green Lantern and Batman first met during Darkseid's invasion of the Earth. Hal Jordan was surprised to learn that the Dark Knight possessed no special powers, and was simply Bruce Wayne in an armored uniform.

Ring creates Hal's mask and uniform

Responsible for protecting space sector 2814

Green power ring creates anything Hal can imagine

As a child, Hal Jordan idolized his pilot father, who died in a plane crash. Hal grew up to be just like his dad, overcoming his fear of flying and finding work at Ferris Airlines. When Abin Sur, a member of the galactic peacekeepers known as the Green Lanterns, crashed his spaceship on Earth, his magical ring chose Hal to replace Abin Sur as the newest member of the Green Lanterns.

"You're not just some guy in a bat costume, are you?"

THE FLASH

VITAL STATS

Real Name: Barry Allen

Occupation: Hero, forensic scientist

Height: 5ft 11in

Weight: 179 lbs

Base: Central City

Allies: The Justice League, Green Lantern, Iris West

Foes: Captain Cold, Mirror Master, Heatwave, Captain Boomerang

POWERS AND ABILITIES

Draws super-speed powers from an extradimensional Speed Force energy; extremely intelligent; well-versed in police procedure and detection; skilled crime scene investigator.

SPEED BUMPS

The Flash has gathered his own Rogues Gallery over the years, from villains like Heatwave, to murderers like the Keystone Killer. As the Flash, and as a crime scene investigator, he does his best to protect his city.

When Barry Allen was a boy, his mother died, and his father was arrested as the culprit. Desperate to get to the truth, Barry studied forensics, and later became a criminologist for the police. One night, a bolt of lightning struck a shelf of chemicals, splashing them onto Allen, giving him the power to move at fantastic speeds as the Flash.

"No matter what—I'll never stop chasing the truth."

Designed his own flame-colored costume

Costume can shrink small enough to fit inside a ring

Speed causes lightning to trail off behind him

GREEN ARROW

HERO

VITAL STATS

Real Name: Oliver Queen

Occupation: Hero, head of the Queen Foundation

Height: 5ft 11in

Weight: 185 lbs

Base: Seattle, Washington

Allies: The Justice League of America, Katana, Arsenal, Batman

Foes: Count Vertigo, Richard Dragon II, the Clock King

POWERS AND ABILITIES

Expert archer with variety of arrows; skilled hand-to-hand combatant and martial artist.

TAKING AIM

During his crime-fighting career, Green Arrow has amassed his own Rogues Gallery, from the team of Midas and Blood Rose, to the master martial artist Richard Dragon and the gang leader, the Clock King.

Heir to the Queen fortune, Oliver Queen lived a life of excess. Despite being trained from an early age in the art of the bow and arrow by his father, Robert, Oliver didn't embrace the skill until he was stranded on a deserted island for three years. Oliver eventually escaped from the island, and reemerged in Seattle a changed man, fighting criminals as the hero Green Arrow.

"I won't let anyone else get hurt in this city because of me."

Quiver filled with array of trick arrows

Belt contains small crime-fighting tools

Armored suit helps protect from damage

Bow also used as handle for zip lines

Shins and forearms have added armor

MARTIAN MANHUNTER

VITAL STATS

Real Name: J'onn J'onzz

Occupation: Hero

Height: 6ft 7in

Weight: 250 lbs

Base: Mobile

Allies: The Justice League of America, the Justice League, Stormwatch, the Justice League United

Foes: The Crime Syndicate, the Secret Society

POWERS AND ABILITIES

Super-strength; super-speed; superhuman agility and endurance; invisibility; shape-shifting powers; flight; telepathy; Martian vision; able to pass through solid objects; highly intelligent and determined; natural leader.

SUPER-MANHUNTER

The Martian Manhunter is one of the most powerful Super Heroes. Possessing most of the abilities of Superman, J'onn's shape-shifting, telepathy, and invisibility powers give him a huge advantage in any fight.

Can communicate with others by thought

Green skin a sign of Martian heritage

Costume can shape-shift with his flesh

Body can pass through solid objects

The people of Mars lived a connected life, communicating with each other through their thoughts. When J'onn J'onzz became their leader, he journeyed to another world to experience the feeling of being alone. When he returned he found Mars aflame. Believing he was the planet's sole survivor, he traveled to Earth to use his powers for good as the Martian Manhunter.

"My friends call me J'onn..."

LEX LUTHOR

VITAL STATS

Full Name: Lex Luthor

Occupation: CEO of LexCorp, criminal

Height: 6ft 2in

Weight: 210 lbs

Base: Metropolis

Allies: Captain Cold, the Justice League, Mercy Graves, Brainiac

Foes: Superman, the Crime Syndicate, Batman

POWERS AND ABILITIES

Near unparalleled intellect; armored flight suit equipped with hi-tech weaponry and defenses; suit grants him superhuman strength and speed.

INJUSTICE FOR ALL

After convincing the world he was a true hero by playing a major part in the defeat of the Crime Syndicate, Lex Luthor rallied public support to become a member of the Justice League.

Lex Luthor first met Superman whilst working with the United States government and the alien entity known as Brainiac. Wishing to be mankind's savior against the alien threat Superman presented, he helped capture and experiment on the Kryptonian hero but Superman escaped. Luthor has maintained a vendetta against Superman ever since.

"I'm a changed man, Superman."

Genius-level intellect and business savvy

Clothes suit his luxurious lifestyle

Dresses in business attire, when not in hero costume

BLACK LIGHTNING

HERO

VITAL STATS

Real Name: Jefferson Pierce

Occupation: Hero,
high school teacher

Height: 6ft 1in

Weight: 200 lbs

Base: Los Angeles,
California

Allies: Batman, Blue Devil,
the Justice League,

Foe: Tobias Whale

POWERS AND ABILITIES

Can generate black
electricity from his own
body; Olympic-level athlete;
natural leader; excellent
teacher with a very
intelligent mind.

BLACK AND BLUE
Black Lightning has been
known to team with the
magical hero Blue Devil.
Before the two were
Super Hero partners,
they were old high school
friends who played on
the same football team.

Jefferson Pierce's father is a reporter
who instilled a strong sense of right
and wrong in his son. Jefferson grew
up to become an Olympic gold medalist
in track and field, and later evolved
into the electricity-powered hero Black
Lightning. He formed a partnership
with Blue Devil and was even recruited
by Batman and the Justice League,
but chose not to become a member.

*"Never lose your focus
in a fight!"*

Visor hides
identity and
protects eyes

Costume
can generate
electricity too

Altered costume
to include gold
design

THE OUTSIDERS

VITAL STATS

Team Name: The Outsiders

Base: Gotham City

Allies: Batman, Batman, Inc., Alfred Pennyworth

Foes: Mr. Freeze, Clayface, Leviathan, Masters of Disaster

Notable Members:
Geo-Force, Halo, Katana, Metamorpho, Black Lightning, Looker, Red Robin, Freight Train, Owlman (Roy Raymond, Jr.)

OUTSIDE HELP

When Batman was sent time traveling by the villain Darkseid, Alfred Pennyworth decided to unite his allies, the Outsiders, into a new team to pick up where the Dark Knight left off.

The team of Super Heroes called the Outsiders has shared a long history with Batman and his allies. United some time ago as Batman's personal strike force to go on missions the Justice League wouldn't touch, the Outsiders have proved themselves devoutly loyal to the Caped Crusader, repeatedly putting their lives on the line, even against the evil forces of Leviathan.

"We're a low maintenance crowd."

When uniting against the forces of Leviathan, Batman teamed the Outsiders with their new leader and his former partner, Red Robin.

KATANA

VITAL STATS

Real Name: Tatsu Toro

Occupation: Hero, assassin

Height: 5ft 2in

Weight: 96 lbs

Base: Japantown, San Francisco, California

Allies: The Birds of Prey, the Justice League of America, Batman

Foes: The Creeper, Coil, Killer Croc

POWERS AND ABILITIES

Skilled martial artist with expertise in swordsmanship; communicates with deceased inhabitants of her sword.

OUTSIDER ON THE INSIDE

Katana is often at odds with the Sword Clan crime family, including its deadly member Coil. She allied herself briefly with the Swords, but was never an official member as she was with the Justice League of America and the Birds of Prey.

Tatsu Toro was torn between her husband, Maseo Yamashiro, and his brother, Takeo, a martial artist. During a fight between them, Tatsu stepped in, accidentally killing Maseo and trapping his soul in the Soultaker sword. Tatsu dedicated her life to fighting and swordsmanship as Katana, maintaining a relationship with Maseo's trapped soul.

Soultaker sword traps the souls of its victims

Wears colors of Japan's flag on her mask

Armored suit provides full-body protection

Armored patch protects against swords

Lightweight suit worn under casual clothing

"...I am not here to make friends."

METAMORPHO

HERO

VITAL STATS

Real Name: Rex Mason
Occupation: Hero, adventurer
Height: 6ft 1in
Weight: 200 lbs
Base: Haneyville
Allies: Batman, Inc., the Outsiders, Batman, Sapphire Stagg
Foes: Simon Stagg, Leviathan, Java

POWERS AND ABILITIES

Can transform his body into any element or mix of elements found in the human body; brave explorer with loyal heart; superhuman recovery and endurance; knowledge of ancient artifacts.

CURSE THE ELEMENTS

Despite possessing amazing powers that enable him to turn himself as hard as steel, or as untouchable as a gas, Metamorpho simply wants to return to human form and continue his life with Sapphire Stagg.

An adventurer who loved a challenge, Rex Mason was in love with Sapphire Stagg, daughter of the wealthy and corrupt Simon Stagg. While exploring an ancient pyramid, Rex was betrayed by Stagg's henchman and exposed to a meteor that changed him into Metamorpho, the Element Man. He put his powers to good use as a member of Batman's Outsiders team.

"Always one step a—head."

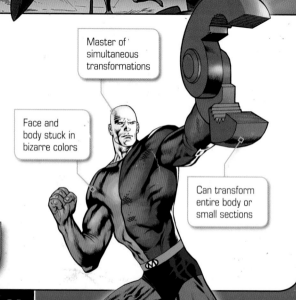

Master of simultaneous transformations

Face and body stuck in bizarre colors

Can transform entire body or small sections

GEO-FORCE

VITAL STATS

Real Name: Brion Markov
Occupation: Ruler of Markovia
Height: 6ft 4in
Weight: 210 lbs
Base: Markovia
Allies: The Outsiders, Batman, Terra
Foes: Masters of Disaster, Clayface, Baron Bedlam

POWERS AND ABILITIES

Projects lava blasts from hands; can increase or decrease gravity on himself or others; combines lava blast and gravity powers to propel himself via flight; superhuman strength, endurance, and durability; able to manipulate earth and rock.

MOVER AND SHAKER

Due to the evil schemes of the villain Deathstroke, Geo-Force gained the ability of a so-called "earth-mover." This means he is able to control and manipulate rocks and dirt, abilities that complement his gravity powers.

The Prince of the Eastern European nation of Markovia, Brion Markov had a bright future ahead of him. A keen patriot, he volunteered himself for an experiment that gave him earth-themed powers. He adopted the identity of Geo-Force and became a founding member of the Outsiders. He is a loyal ally of the Dark Knight when not serving his country as its ruler.

"...isn't it time for evil to be punished?"

Brion became ruler of Markovia after the death of his brother. He now has the ability to protect his people from the throne and on the battlefield.

HALO

VITAL STATS

Real Name: Gabrielle Doe

Occupation: Hero

Height: 5ft 7in

Weight: 120 lbs

Base: Mobile

Allies: The Outsiders, Batman, Inc., Batman

Foes: Leviathan, Talia al Ghūl, Syonide II

POWERS AND ABILITIES

Controls and manipulates visible energy, called an aura: red aura generates heat; orange aura projects force blasts; yellow aura generates light; green aura keeps things still; blue distortion aura causes illusions; indigo aura is a tractor beam; all auras enable flight and space travel.

GROWING PAINS

As a member of the Outsiders, Halo matured from a naïve girl to a strong and independent young woman, often guided by the woman she saw as a mother figure, Katana.

Before Batman gave her the name Halo, the woman who would adopt the name of Gabrielle Doe wasn't a woman at all, but an Aurakle, a cosmic being from a race older than time itself. Curious about human life, this Aurakle reached out to a dying girl, Violet Harper, and found herself trapped in the girl's human form. She forgot her own past for a time and became Halo.

"Halo here. Everything's okay."

Halo's green aura is her stasis aura. It can freeze any living thing or chemical reaction in place, but it doesn't work on machines or affect gravity.

SHAZAM!

VITAL STATS

Real Name: Billy Batson

Occupation: Hero, student

Height: 6ft 1in

Weight: 195 lbs

Base: Philadelphia

Allies: The Justice League, Freddy Freeman

Foes: Black Adam, Mazahs, Dr. Sivana, Mr. Mind

POWERS AND ABILITIES

Superhuman wisdom, courage, strength, endurance, agility, speed, senses, and durability; flight; ability to call down magic lightning; can transform from teen to adult by saying the magic word, "Shazam!"

BLACK MAGIC

With one word, "Shazam!", teenager Billy Batson is transformed into a mystically-powered adult, controlling the power of living lightning. His abilities came in handy when forced to combat his would-be usurper, Black Adam.

Can share magic with others if he so chooses

An orphan, 15-year-old Billy Batson was taken in by the kindly Vasquez family. One night, the subway car Billy was riding in magically took him to the Rock of Eternity where he met an old wizard. The wizard turned him into the Super Hero Shazam! After facing down the threat of villain Black Adam, Shazam put his powers to good use by joining the Justice League.

Magic lightning bolt symbol constantly glows

Costume appears when he transforms

"You picked the wrong person to push around."

VITAL STATS

Team Name: The Justice League of America

Base: A.R.G.U.S. headquarters, Washington, D.C.

Allies: The Justice League, Amanda Waller

Foes: The Secret Society, the Crime Syndicate

Members: Colonel Steve Trevor, Catwoman, Katana, Green Arrow, Hawkman, Stargirl, Martian Manhunter, Green Lantern Simon Baz, Vibe, Dr. Light

BOXING MATCH

Shortly after the Justice League of America formed, they fought the original Justice League over a relic called Pandora's Box. What they didn't realize was that the box opened a portal to the nefarious dimension Earth-Three.

Worried that the Justice League did not operate under government control, the US government directed Amanda Waller to create an official US Super Hero team. Waller recruited Steve Trevor to lead the all-new Justice League of America. Ready to take down the original Justice League if required, the JLA was the country's first line of defense against superhuman threats.

"We introduce the JLA to the world tomorrow."

With the teen icon Stargirl a member, the team was welcomed onto the Super Hero scene by the masses.

THE TEEN TITANS

VITAL STATS

Team Name: The Teen Titans

Base: New York City

Allies: The Batman Family, the Outlaws, S.T.A.R. Labs

Foes: Harvest, Trigon, Deathstroke

Members: Red Robin, Bunker, Beast Boy, Raven, Superboy, Wonder Girl (former), Power Girl (former), Kid Flash (former), Solstice (former), Skitter (former), Danny the Alley (former)

S.T.A.R.S OF THE SHOW

When there's trouble, call the Teen Titans. The latest incarnation of the team began working hand in hand with the scientifically advanced S.T.A.R. Labs and includes Beast Boy, Red Robin, Bunker, and Raven.

When teen heroes were being captured by a villain called Harvest, Red Robin decided to recruit young metahumans and form a team of Super Heroes to combat the threat. He enlisted the help of Wonder Girl and other young heroes, including Kid Flash and Bunker. Together, they ended Harvest's reign of terror, and the team continues to fight injustice as the Teen Titans.

"Maybe we can do great things together."

Once an important member of the Teen Titans, Wonder Girl quit its ranks to lead a morally questionable team called the Elite.

THE OUTLAWS

VITAL STATS

Team Name: The Outlaws
Base: Unnamed, uncharted island
Allies: Batman, the Batman Family, Crux
Foes: Rā's al Ghūl, the Untitled, Suzie Su

Members:
Red Hood
Arsenal
Starfire

AN ATTACK ON CRIME
The Outlaws often chose to pursue figures from the world of organized crime. One such unlucky individual was the Hong Kong crime lord known as Suzie Su, who didn't survive their last encounter.

Green Arrow's former partner Arsenal was imprisoned in in the eastern nation of Qura. He was rescued by the Super Hero Red Hood and Starfire, an alien princess from the planet Tamaran. The three set up a base in Starfire's marooned starship, forming a team called the Outlaws. Starfire later quit, leaving Red Hood and Arsenal to form a partnership.

Starfire, aka Princess Koriand'r

Arsenal, aka Roy Harper

Red Hood, aka Jason Todd

"We were friends, helping each other...we were outlaws!"

RAGMAN

VITAL STATS

Real Name: Rory Regan

Occupation: Hero, pawnshop owner

Height: 5ft 11in

Weight: 165 lbs

Base: Gotham City

_____ woman, the
Un___ Batman

Foe: ___ine le Fey

POWERS AND ABILITIES

Wears suit of rags composed of evil souls; can absorb souls into his suit in order to stop corrupt individuals; granted strengths and knowledge of those imprisoned in his rags; superhuman agility, speed, and strength; can float on air currents.

RAGTIME

The mysterious Ragman has teamed up with Batman in the past, and became a staunch ally of Batwoman as a fellow member of the Unknowns. He was integral in the defeat of evil sorceress Morgaine le Fey.

By day, the owner of the Rags 'n' Tatters pawnshop in Gotham City, Rory Regan does his best to help his neighbors in tough times. By night, he patrols the city in a mystical living suit of rags that summons him when he is needed. Rory's suit is actually a cloth "golem" of sorts, created by an ancient Council of Rabbis to protect the Jewish people.

Constantly struggling with the evil souls within his rags

Suit clothes him when he is needed

Rags surround and speak to him

Can be as light as rags, to float on wind

"I specialize in finding truths."

THE JOKER

VITAL STATS

Real Name: Unknown

Occupation: Criminal

Height: 6ft 5in

Weight: 192 lbs

Base: Gotham City

Allies: Harley Quinn, the Joker's Daughter, the Red Hood Gang

Foes: Batman, the Batman Family, James Gordon

POWERS AND ABILITIES

Insanity causes unpredictable behavior; agile and a relentless fighter; twisted genius mind with expertise in chemistry; brilliant strategist; lacks moral code; employs clown-themed weapons; Venom gives his victims permanent grins.

KILLER CLOWN FROM GOTHAM CITY

The Joker considers himself Batman's arch-enemy, and is virtually obsessed with the hero and his team. During his career, he has temporarily paralyzed Batgirl and killed Jason Todd, and even severed Alfred's hand.

While his true identity remains a mystery, the Joker is believed to have been the criminal known as Red Hood One, the man in charge of the Red Hood Gang. That chapter of his life ended when Batman took down his organization and knocked the criminal into a vat of chemicals. The Joker survived, albeit with severely altered features, including a damaged mind.

Uses razor-sharp playing cards as weapons

Hair dyed green from chemical exposure

Trademark purple suit with clashing shirt and tie

Employs deadly "jokes" like acid-squirting flowers

"Just think of the great times we've had...and smile!"

HARLEY QUINN

ROGUE

VITAL STATS

Real Name: Dr. Harleen Quinzel

Occupation: Criminal, landlord, roller derby participant

Height: 5ft 7in

Weight: 115 lbs

Base: Coney Island, Brooklyn, New York

Allies: The Joker, Suicide Squad, Poison Ivy, Scarecrow

Foes: Batman, the Batman Family

POWERS AND ABILITIES

Insanity causes unpredictability; agile and capable fighter; employs dozens of clown-themed weapons and lackeys; often uses giant hammer as a weapon.

LEFT HER HEART IN GOTHAM CITY

Putting Gotham City and her love affair with the Joker behind her, Harley Quinn moved to Coney Island and set up shop as a landlord, taking part in roller derbies.

Harley Quinn was a Gotham University graduate who began working at Arkham Asylum. To gain the inmates' trust, she dyed her hair two-toned and posed as a patient. The Joker saw through her ruse, and Harley found herself falling in love with him. They escaped Arkham, and the Joker threw her into a vat of chemicals to bleach her skin and cement their relationship.

"Oh, Mistah J..."

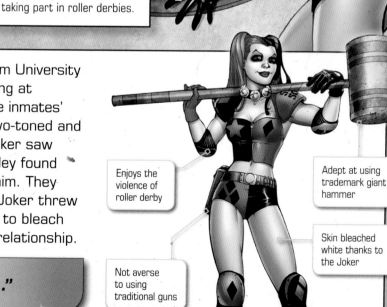

Enjoys the violence of roller derby

Adept at using trademark giant hammer

Skin bleached white thanks to the Joker

Not averse to using traditional guns

THE PENGUIN

VITAL STATS

Real Name: Oswald
Chesterfield Cobblepot
Occupation: Crime boss,
owner of the Iceberg Casino
Height: 5ft 2in
Weight: 175 lbs
Base: Gotham City
Allies: Lark, Catwoman,
Mr. Toxic, Hypnotic,
Mr. Combustible
Foes: Batman, the Batman
Family, Black Canary

POWERS AND ABILITIES

Master strategist;
brilliant criminal mind;
employs a variety of
trick umbrellas; major
underworld connections.

OLD ENEMIES

Batman and the Penguin have
a long history, going back to a
time before either of them had
adopted their animal-themed
names. Batman often takes
advantage of the Penguin's
extensive criminal ties, scaring
information out of the villain.

White gloves
coordinate
with the spats
on his shoes

Physical features
resemble a
penguin

Weapons are
concealed in
his umbrellas

Agile and violent
despite his size

Oswald Chesterfield Cobblepot hails
from one of Gotham City's oldest
and most influential families, albeit a
corrupt one. Determined to climb to
the top of the heap, Oswald continued
his family's legacy, dealing in illegal
weapons. Now known as the Penguin,
he rose to power in Gotham City's
underworld, becoming a feared crime
boss and owner of the Iceberg Casino.

*"Almost everything went
according to plan, little birdie."*

POISON IVY

VITAL STATS

Real Name: Pamela
Lillian Isley
Occupation: Criminal,
eco-terrorist
Height: 5ft 8in
Weight: 115 lbs
Base: Gotham City
Allies: Harley Quinn, Clayface,
the Justice League United
Foes: Batman, the Batman
Family, the Birds of Prey

POWERS AND ABILITIES

Controls and manipulates
growth of plants; immune to
toxins and poisons; produces
pheromones that cause
others to fall into her control;
poisonous kiss; highly adept
at botany and chemistry.

TANGLED IN IVY

Poison Ivy and Batman have clashed
frequently, but they first butted heads
when Isley worked briefly for Wayne
Enterprises. She was fired for
developing a mind-controlling pheromone
that Bruce Wayne found immoral.

As a girl, Pamela Isley was adept at
chemistry and developed a deadly toxin
in her mother's garden that she could
deliver to her enemies with a kiss.
When she was accidentally doused
with an experimental plant-based serum
during a struggle in her lab, she gained
the ability to communicate with nature.
She soon set out to exploit that power
as the eco-terrorist, Poison Ivy.

*"Are you scared,
little mammal?"*

Can "speak"
to plants and
control them

Highly intelligent,
with a mind for
chemistry

Body changes
with seasons
like a true
plant

Wears plant-
based living
costume

TWO-FACE

VITAL STATS

Real Name: Harvey Dent

Occupation: Criminal, former District Attorney

Height: 6ft

Weight: 182 lbs

Base: Gotham City

Allies: The Secret Society, Gilda Dent

Foes: Batman, the Batman Family, Erin McKillen

POWERS AND ABILITIES

Cunning strategist; expert knowledge of law and police procedure; split personality causes extreme unpredictability.

TWO SIDES OF THE SAME COIN
Harvey Dent and his old friend Bruce Wayne have become enemies as Two-Face and Batman. With a flip of his special coin, Two-Face lets luck dictate his every decision—good or evil.

Gotham City's District Attorney, Harvey Dent, led a promising life as the city's golden boy. But when he crossed Erin McKillen of the organized crime family known as the McKillen Clan, his life changed forever. Erin took revenge upon Harvey and his family. The trauma of this tragic event released Harvey's dark side, and he took on the persona of the criminal Two-Face.

Scarred two-headed coin to match his face

Handsome features are now forever marred

Wears two-toned clothing

*"Chance **trumps** choice **every second of every day**."*

THE JOKER'S DAUGHTER

ROGUE

VITAL STATS

Real Name: Duela Dent

Occupation: Criminal, leader of underground cult

Height: 5ft 4in

Weight: 120 lbs

Base: Gotham City

Allies: Suicide Squad

Foes: Catwoman, Batman, Batgirl

POWERS AND ABILITIES

Criminal mastermind; uses the Joker's urban legend to her advantage; manic fighter; employs moon-shaped blade for combat.

CLOWN PRINCESS

The Joker's Daughter gained followers when she took control of an underground tribe in the Nethers. Obsessed with the Joker, she has run afoul of Batman, Catwoman, and Batgirl in her short criminal career.

Duela was a disturbed young woman living with her family in the Gotham City suburbs. After her face was scarred during a botched surgery, she fled for the grime and squalor of Gotham City's underground tunnels. There she discovered the Joker's lost skin mask. In a grab for power, she adopted it as her own face, becoming the so-called Joker's Daughter.

"Hit me like one of your super-villains, Batman!"

Clad in the Joker's colors: purple and green

Wears the Joker's skin as a mask

Staff often has moon-shaped blade

Shirt design implies the Joker is her father

BANE

ROGUE

VITAL STATS

Real Name: Unknown

Occupation: Criminal

Height: 6ft 8in

Weight: 350 lbs (425 lbs on Venom)

Base: Gotham City

Allies: Santa Prisca mercenaries

Foes: Batman, the Batman Family, Batwoman

POWERS AND ABILITIES

Extremely intelligent with an iron-clad will; brilliant strategist; skilled hand-to-hand fighter; enhanced strength, durability, weight, and endurance due to use of super-steroid Venom.

BREAKING BAT

Bane lives with one goal in mind: to break the Batman. Bane had heard legends of the Dark Knight while in his native country of Santa Prisca, and yearned to conquer the seemingly untamable Gotham City and its dark protector.

Born in the corrupt nation of Santa Prisca, the boy who would become Bane grew up in its cruelest prison, Pena Duro, becoming a hardened yet well-read man. The prison doctors injected him with a powerful steroid called Venom. Not only did the steroid work, it gave Bane the strength he needed to escape and set his sights on Gotham City.

"Only when I'm dead do I intend to rest."

Always equipped with Venom supply

Venom injected directly into head

Often leads army of Santa Prisca soldiers

Huge exterior can overshadow brilliant mind

CLAYFACE

VITAL STATS

Real Name: Basil Karlo

Occupation: Criminal, former actor

Height: Varies

Weight: Varies

Base: Gotham City

Allies: Poison Ivy, the Unknowns, Batwoman

Foes: Batman, the Batman Family

POWERS AND ABILITIES

Made of living clay that can bend and shape to his will; able to impersonate others by taking their exact shape and DNA; highly skilled actor.

IMPRESSIONABLE

While Clayface has primarily been an enemy of Batman, he briefly joined forces with Batwoman and a team called the Unknowns when he suffered from amnesia. He has since reverted to his criminal ways.

Basil Karlo was a famous actor, known primarily for his roles in horror films. However, when replaced as the lead in a movie, he turned to murder. His life began to take a strange path when he injected himself with a formula that altered his body completely, making him a shape-changer made of living clay. He became Clayface, one of Batman's most powerful enemies.

> "...I ain't your daddy's Clayface!"

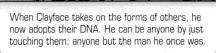

When Clayface takes on the forms of others, he now adopts their DNA. He can be anyone by just touching them; anyone but the man he once was.

RĀ'S AL GHŪL

ROGUE

VITAL STATS

Real Name: Unknown
Occupation: International terrorist
Height: 6ft 5in
Weight: 215 lbs
Base: 'Eth Alth'eban
Allies: The League of Assassins, Talia al Ghūl
Foes: Batman, Robin, the Batman Family

POWERS AND ABILITIES

Extremely long-life through his unprecedented access to the anti-aging Lazarus Pits; expert swordsman; highly skilled martial artist and fighter; genius intellect; master strategist.

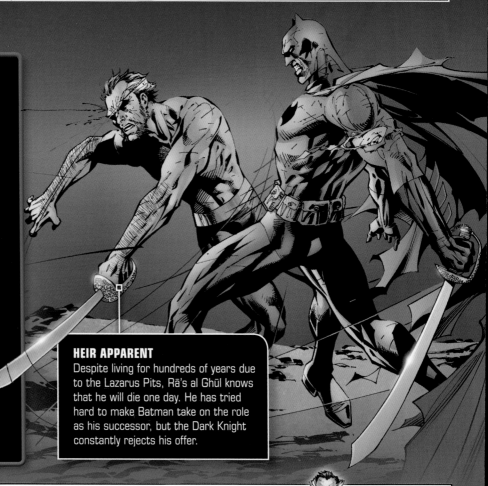

HEIR APPARENT

Despite living for hundreds of years due to the Lazarus Pits, Rā's al Ghūl knows that he will die one day. He has tried hard to make Batman take on the role as his successor, but the Dark Knight constantly rejects his offer.

Legend tells of Rā's al Ghūl walking the Earth for the last 700 years. He adopted the name "The Demon's Head" after the death of his wife. Prolonging his own life through restorative Lazarus Pits, Rā's has amassed an entire League of Assassins with the goal of destroying the majority of the population in order to shape the world in his cruel image.

Speaks many different languages

Aging slowed thanks to Lazarus Pits

Ornate gold detailing

Wears regal clothing fit for a ruler

"My League of Assassins will tear this world apart..."

TALIA AL GHUL

ROGUE

VITAL STATS

Full Name: Talia al Ghūl

Occupation: International terrorist

Height: 5ft 8in

Weight: 120 lbs

Base: Mobile

Allies: Rā's al Ghūl, Leviathan, Red Hood, the League of Assassins

Foes: Batman, Robin, the Batman Family, Batman, Inc.

POWERS AND ABILITIES

Access to huge terrorist networks; superb fighter and assassin; extremely intelligent with a mind for strategy; charismatic leader; worked her way into both Batman and Robin's hearts.

IN THE NAME OF THE FATHER

While she stayed by his side for years, Talia al Ghūl later parted ways with her father. She formed her own terrorist organization called Leviathan, and set out to destroy Batman once and for all.

Talia al Ghūl is the daughter of the terrorist Rā's al Ghūl, and grew up learning the evil methods of being an assassin. When she met Batman, the two were instantly attracted to one another and had a short-lived romance that resulted in the birth of their son, Damian Wayne. While leading the criminal organization Leviathan, Talia was shot and presumably killed.

> **"Look into the eye of the gorgon."**

Uses laboratories for immoral experiments

Beauty causes some to drop their guard

Wears expensive regal attire

THE LEAGUE OF ASSASSINS

VITAL STATS

Team Name: The League of Assassins

Base: 'Eth Alth'eban

Allies: Rā's al Ghūl, Talia al Ghūl, Red Hood

Foes: Batman, the Batman Family, Deathstroke, the Untitled

Notable Members:
Rā's al Ghūl, Talia al Ghūl, Lady Shiva, Bronze Tiger, Cheshire, December Graystone, Rictus, Dr. Darrk, Red Hood (former), Anya Volkova (former)

EVE OF DESTRUCTION
Always pursuing immortality, Rā's al Ghūl sent the League of Assassins to Mother Eve, hoping to learn the secret of her de-aging process. Fortunately, Batgirl and the Birds of Prey were on hand to defend their ally.

Formed by the international terrorist Rā's al Ghūl, the League of Assassins is an elite and clandestine organization based in the mystical city of 'Eth Alth'eban. The League is usually led by Rā's, whose ultimate goal is to destroy a significant portion of the world's population in order to shape what is left into a world of his choosing.

"We are the League of Assassins. We are death incarnate."

Rā's al Ghūl takes a hands-on approach as leader of the League of Assassins. He is very often present during its missions.

LADY SHIVA

VITAL STATS

Real Name: Sandra Wu-San

Occupation: Mercenary

Height: 5ft 8in

Weight: 115 lbs

Base: 'Eth Alth'eban

Allies: The League of Assassins, Rā's al Ghūl, Ninja Man-Bats

Foes: Batman, Dick Grayson, the Untitled

POWERS AND ABILITIES

Arguably the world's greatest martial artist; master of many weapons; commands army of Ninja Man-Bats when working with the League of Assassins; brilliant and cunning mind.

SHIVA THE DESTROYER

When Dick Grayson was Robin, he interrupted a fight between Batman and Lady Shiva. Lady Shiva has the skill to read fighting styles like language, so when she later met Grayson in his Nightwing guise, she instantly recognized him.

Lady Shiva is considered one of the world's greatest assassins, and boasts a long history with Batman and his allies. As a member of the League of Assassins, Shiva has worked directly for Rā's al Ghūl, as well as commanded her own missions. Despite working with the League, Lady Shiva is most often found alone, committing one assassination after another.

"Fear us. Fear me. Lady Shiva!"

Even her hair is weaponized with a blade

Thinks several steps ahead of her opponents

Expert at nearly every type of traditional weapon

MR. FREEZE

VITAL STATS

Real Name: Dr. Victor Fries

Occupation: Criminal, former scientist

Height: 6ft

Weight: 190 lbs

Base: Gotham City

Allies: Starling, Scarecrow, Harley Quinn, Merrymaker, Professor Pyg

Foes: Batman, the Batman Family, the Birds of Prey, the Court of Owls

POWERS AND ABILITIES

Refrigerated suit gives him superhuman strength and endurance; developed quick-freeze technology in the form of freeze guns and grenades; genius-level intellect.

ICE IN HIS VEINS

With a body temperature of 23 degrees Fahrenheit, Victor Fries was fitted with special goggles to keep his eyes from freezing. He developed a refrigerated exoskeleton and an arsenal of cold weapons to become Mr. Freeze.

When Victor Fries was just a boy, his mother died in a frozen lake. As an adult, he took a job at Wayne Enterprises' cryogenics lab, where he focused on freezing bodies. He became obsessed with the frozen body of a woman he'd never met, Nora Fields. When Bruce Wayne closed his division, Fries lashed out, causing a lab accident that transformed him into Mr. Freeze.

"You don't understand what you're meddling with, Batman."

Mr. Freeze is obsessed with Nora Fields and believes they were married before she was frozen. He'll kill anyone that hampers finding her a cure.

VITAL STATS

Real Name: Waylon Jones

Occupation: Criminal

Height: 6ft 5in

Weight: 268 lbs

Base: Gotham City

Allies: Arsenal, Catwoman

Foes: Batman, the Batman Family, Bane

POWERS AND ABILITIES

Enhanced strength, durability, and endurance due to rare skin condition; excellent fighter with a history of wrestling alligators.

LURKING IN THE SEWERS

On the surface, Killer Croc can be perceived as simple muscle, but in the sewers he commands respect. Croc knows the underground inside and out, and has even ruled over tribes of vagabonds. He is known to them as King Croc.

Teeth filed to sharp points

Extremely strong and muscular

Skin tough and difficult to pierce

Waylon Jones was raised by his Aunt Flowers in the poor neighborhood of Crown Point in Gotham City. Born with a skin condition that caused scale growth all over his body, Waylon knew no other life aside from one in a circus sideshow. Frustrated with his low pay and, after biting his employer while in a rage, Jones ventured into a life of crime as Killer Croc.

"Death by Croc."

CARMINE FALCONE

VITAL STATS

Full Name: Carmine Falcone

Occupation: Crime boss

Height: 6ft 1in

Weight: 205 lbs

Base: Gotham City

Allies: Mayor Sebastian Hady, Jack Forbes, Tiger Shark

Foes: Batman, Catwoman, James Gordon, the Penguin

POWERS AND ABILITIES

Powerful crime boss; highly connected in Gotham City's underworld; amassed wealth through illegal means; intelligent, strategic mind; years of criminal experience.

ET TU, CATWOMAN?

During Batman's campaign to drive Falcone out of Gotham City, Catwoman lashed out at the crime boss, scarring his face with her claws. Falcone has sought revenge against Catwoman ever since.

It took the combined efforts of Batman and James Gordon to run the organized crime boss Carmine "the Roman" Falcone out of Gotham City. So when Falcone returned to the city when Gordon was wrongly imprisoned, it was certainly cause for concern. Carmine's second stay in Gotham City was cut short, however, when he was arrested by the G.C.P.D.'s Jason Bard.

Carmine Falcone is good at making enemies. He was once abducted by Professor Pyg and his animal-masked gang before Batman saved his life.

"This city won't let me lose."

REX "THE LION" CALABRESE

ROGUE

VITAL STATS

Full Name: Rex Calabrese

Occupation: Former crime boss

Height: 6ft

Weight: 265 lbs

Base: Gotham City

Allies: Catwoman, the Calabrese Crime family

Foes: Carmine Falcone, Batman, the Penguin

POWERS AND ABILITIES

Powerful former crime boss; highly connected in Gotham City's underworld; amassed wealth through illegal means; intelligent, strategic mind; years of criminal experience.

LUCK OF THE LION

Named "Leo" by fellow inmates, Calabrese has spent the last several years in Blackgate Penitentiary. His former protégé, Carmine Falcone, thought he had killed Calabrese, and had no idea he was hiding in jail.

Rex "The Lion" Calabrese was once one of the most powerful underworld figures in Gotham City. His career was thought to be cut short when he was "killed" by a former ally. In reality, Rex was in hiding, and eventually made contact with his daughter, Selina Kyle, to persuade her to take over the family crime business. She agreed, although she harbored many angry feelings toward him.

> *"The cat's outta the bag, so to speak."*

When Catwoman's father first approached her to unite Gotham City's crime families, she lashed out, angry that he had abandoned her.

ANTHONY ZUCCO

VITAL STATS

Full Name: Anthony Zucco
Occupation: Criminal, former mayor's aide
Height: 6ft
Weight: 240 lbs
Base: Chicago
Ally: Mayor Wallace Cole
Foes: Dick Grayson, Sophia Branch, Prankster, Batman

POWERS AND ABILITIES

Intelligent strategist; many criminal connections in the Gotham City underworld and in Chicago; personal friend of the mayor of Chicago; uses firearm.

ACCEPTING RESPONSIBILITY

Tony Zucco attempted to turn his life around in Chicago, assuming the fake name Billy Lester, marrying, and having a child. When Nightwing tracked him down, Zucco finally came clean and admitted his guilt.

Tony Zucco was a shakedown artist with plans to make a name for himself. When attempting to gain protection money from Haly's Circus, Zucco threatened C.C. Haly, a crime a young Dick Grayson witnessed. So when Dick's parents were murdered during their trapeze routine, he knew who the culprit was. Dick hunted Zucco, but the criminal faked his own death.

"...what I did to the Graysons... there's no excuse I can make."

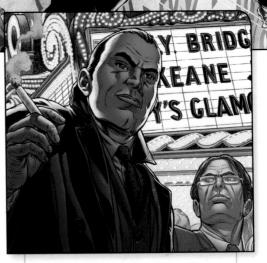

Tony Zucco did much harm in Gotham City. His daughter, however, distanced herself from him by changing her name to Sonia Branch.

JOE CHILL

VITAL STATS

Full Name: Joe Chill
Occupation: Criminal
Height: 5ft 8in
Weight: 180 lbs
Base: Gotham City
Allies: Unknown
Foes: Batman, Thomas and Martha Wayne

POWERS AND ABILITIES

Common street criminal with access to a handgun.

CHILL OF THE NIGHT

Joe Chill happened upon the Waynes when they were exiting a movie on Gotham City's Park Row. He was startled by Martha Wayne's scream, and shot her and her husband.

When young Bruce Wayne's parents were gunned down before his eyes, his life was forever changed. Although he suspected the Court of Owls or some other nefarious organization of being the culprit, he later learned the killer was Joe Chill, after a witness identified the murderer. Bruce tracked Chill to his apartment, to discover not a mastermind, but a petty criminal.

"I didn't mean to."

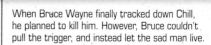

When Bruce Wayne finally tracked down Chill, he planned to kill him. However, Bruce couldn't pull the trigger, and instead let the sad man live.

THE COURT OF OWLS

VITAL STATS

Team Name: The Court of Owls

Base: Gotham City

Allies: Army of Talons and fellow secret Owl members

Foes: Batman, Bane, Talon (Calvin Rose), Lincoln March

Notable Past Members: Benjamin Orchard, John Wycliffe, Maria Powers, Joseph Powers, Sebastian Clark, Lincoln March

GRIPPED BY TALONS
Batman mistakenly suspected the Court of Owls was behind his parents' murder. He first encountered the Court when he was trapped in their labyrinth beneath Gotham City, and he barely managed to escape.

A cult as old as Gotham City itself, the Court of Owls is a secret society of the most nefarious order. Clandestinely controlling politics and the evolution of the city from behind closed doors, the Court employs an elite army of Talons —loyal assassins who murder their enemies from the shadows. Batman stopped a troubling resurgence, but the Court is still alive in Gotham City.

> *"...Beware the Court of Owls, that watches all the time..."*

Members wear owl masks to hide identities

Children brainwashed at young age

Order members are typically society's richest

ROGUE

VITAL STATS

Real Name: William Cobb

Occupation: Assassin for the Court of Owls

Height: 6ft 3in

Weight: 220 lbs

Base: Gotham City

Allies: The Court of Owls

Foes: Batman, Dick Grayson, the Batman Family

POWERS AND ABILITIES

Expertly trained assassin; natural fighter and trained martial artist; superb at knife throwing; has healing ability and can be resurrected from the dead; long-lived and experienced.

CAPE VS. CLAW

When Bruce Wayne was targeted by Talon, Batman began investigating the Court of Owls. This led him to discover the Court's labyrinth, where he was forced to combat Cobb and just barely triumphed over him to escape.

William Cobb, one of the Court of Owls's finest Talon assassins, is the great-grandfather of Dick Grayson. Growing up poor on the streets of Gotham City in the early 1900s, Cobb was recruited into Haly's Circus where he became an expert knife handler. Cobb soon became a Talon for the Court of Owls, later offering his "gray son" to Haly's Circus for training.

"Bruce Wayne. The Court of Owls has sentenced you to die."

Uses owls and owl imagery to threaten

Wears owl-like enhanced goggles

Expert knife thrower

Each Talon wears a different uniform

113

LINCOLN MARCH

VITAL STATS

Real Name: Unknown

Occupation: Criminal

Height: 6ft 4in

Weight: 230 lbs

Base: Gotham City

Ally: Cluemaster

Foes: Batman, the Court of Owls, the Batman Family

POWERS AND ABILITIES

Skilled combatant; advanced armored Talon suit allows for flight, enhanced strength, and durability; suit is fitted with hi-tech devices; brilliant strategist with powerful underworld connections; healing abilities; can be resurrected from the dead.

MARCH ON GOTHAM CITY

After dying and then being regenerated by the Court of Owls, Lincoln March adopted an owl costume and battled Batman. March wanted to destroy the Dark Knight, but he also killed fellow Owls in order to steal their riches.

Despite his claims to the contrary, the true origin of Lincoln March remains a mystery. He insists he is Thomas Wayne, Jr., Bruce Wayne's younger brother who was believed to have died in a car crash. According to March, he was placed in Willowwood Home for Children by his parents after Martha Wayne's car accident, and was forgotten after their death.

Is taller than his "brother" Batman

Has taken Owls's healing serum to be resurrected

Often trades civilian clothes for Talon suit

*"Brother to brother...
owl to bat!"*

BAT-QUEEN

ROGUE

VITAL STATS

Real Name: Francine Langstrom (Felicity Lee)

Occupation: Criminal and corporate spy

Height: 5ft 11in

Weight: 169 lbs

Base: Gotham City

Ally: The Wrath

Foes: Man-Bat, Batman, G.C.P.D.

POWERS AND ABILITIES

Serum transforms her into a monstrous She-Bat with enhanced strength, speed, agility, and endurance, with capability of flight; controls army of piranha-like bats; manipulative and ruthless.

QUEEN OF THE NIGHT

As the villain Bat-Queen, Francine Langstrom's main opposition was her husband, Kirk. Angered that his wife had married him under false pretenses, Kirk wanted nothing more than to put an end to his wife's wicked ways.

The wife of Dr. Kirk Langstrom, who would become Man-Bat, Francine Langstrom's real name is Felicity Lee. A spy tasked with keeping an eye on Kirk's scientific work for her boss, E.D. Caldwell, Francine wanted to help her employer create a biological weapon from Kirk's findings. Creating her own imperfect Man-Bat formula, Francine became the highly unstable Bat-Queen.

High frequency sounds leave her disorientated

Sharpened claws can easily tear through flesh

Stronger than Man-Bat himself

> *"...I am—the Bat-Queen! Screeeee!"*

BRONZE TIGER

VITAL STATS

Real Name: Ben Turner
Occupation: Mercenary
Height: 5ft 11in
Weight: 196 lbs
Base: 'Eth Alth'eban
Allies: Rā's al Ghūl, the League of Assassins, Deathstroke
Foes: The Untitled, Batman

POWERS AND ABILITIES

One of the world's best martial artists; proficient in a variety of fighting styles and weapons; contacts in the espionage and criminal worlds; access to the League of Assassins's assets; able to shift into animalistic tiger form; often wears tiger-themed armor into battle.

TIGER STYLE

An old drinking buddy of Deathstroke's, the Bronze Tiger nevertheless agreed to kill his friend when his mind was being manipulated. Despite working directly with fellow assassin Lady Shiva on this mission, the Tiger was unsuccessful.

Ben Turner is a ranking member of the clandestine mercenary group, the League of Assassins. His ability to transform into a tiger is a useful asset, although it comes at a price. When the vigilante Red Hood was recruited to briefly lead the group, the Bronze Tiger welcomed him. While it is known that he is Deathstroke's old friend, his past remains a mystery.

"Do yourself a favor and yield."

The Bronze Tiger has a talisman that "burns away" at his soul every time he transforms into a tiger. Nonetheless, he often finds it useful in a fight.

DR. DARRK

ROGUE

VITAL STATS

Real Name: Dr. Ebenezer Darcel

Occupation: Criminal

Height: 7ft 4in

Weight: 386 lbs

Base: Mobile

Allies: The League of Assassins, Rā's al Ghūl

Foes: Batman, Talon, Lord Death Man

POWERS AND ABILITIES

Forced to live in a cybernetic body that allows him superhuman strength, endurance, and durability; highly intelligent; access to the assets of the League of Assassins.

LORDING OVER DEATH

As Rā's al Ghūl's employee, the now cybernetically-enhanced Dr. Darrk attempted to mine the secret of Lord Death Man's immortality by extracting the so-called Shelley Formula from his very blood.

When Batman first met Talia al Ghūl, the two became allies when he rescued her from the clutches of Dr. Darrk. While Batman had no idea that Talia's father, Rā's al Ghūl, was the head of the notorious League of Assassins, and that Dr. Darrk had fallen out with his employer, Batman took Talia's side, and comforted her when it appeared she had shot and killed Dr. Darrk.

Dr. Darrk did not die at Talia's hands. Resurfacing as a member of the League of Assassins, he later attempted to best Batman using hallucinogenic gas.

"I've prepared a welcome for our would-be nemesis, our dark pursuer."

DOLLMAKER

VITAL STATS

Real Name: Barton Mathis
Occupation: Criminal
Height: 6ft 1in
Weight: 169 lbs
Base: Gotham City
Allies: The Joker, the Joker's Daughter, Dollhouse
Foes: Batman, the Batman Family, James Gordon

POWERS AND ABILITIES

Skilled surgeon capable of stitching living and dead bodies together to form gruesome "dolls"; intelligent yet twisted mind.

FAMILY MAN

The Dollmaker has passed on his gruesome pastime to his family members, including his son Bentley and his associates Jack-in-the-Box and Sampson. He also has a daughter called Dollhouse, who once battled Catwoman.

The son of serial killer Wesley Mathis, Barton Mathis watched his father get shot down by James Gordon. Seeking revenge, and now calling himself the Dollmaker, he kidnapped the police commissioner, only to have Batman interrupt his scheme. Dollmaker created his most infamous work of "art" when he cut skin from the Joker's face.

Wears mask made from victims' skin

Gifted surgeon with great medical expertise

"This will only hurt—a lot."

MR. MOSAIC

VITAL STATS

Real Name: Unknown
Occupation: Criminal
Height: 5ft 7in
Weight: 208 lbs
Base: Gotham City
Allies: Emperor Blackgate,
Mr. Combustible,
Imperceptible Man,
Mr. Toxic
Foes: Batman, the
Batman Family, G.C.P.D.

POWERS AND ABILITIES

Has extensive ties in the
political and criminal world;
wealthy, and hires others
to do his dirty work for him.

THE LONG GAME

Mr. Mosaic talks a big game,
but when confronted with physical
danger, he backs down from his
larger-than-life persona quite
quickly. Instead, he bides his
time and looks for an opportunity
for revenge down the line.

Little is known about how Mr. Mosaic
rose to power in Gotham City's
underworld, or even how he developed
his bizarre skin condition. What is
known, however, is that he is very
influential in the criminal scene, and
has worked with Emperor Blackgate.
He raided the docks for the gang leader
while the rest of Gotham City was busy
dealing with Blackgate's Man-Bat virus.

*"Think a hitchhiker with a face
like this can get a ride?"*

Mr. Mosaic was one of the criminals freed
by Bane when the villain organized a massive
breakout at Blackgate Penitentiary.

HUGO STRANGE

VITAL STATS

Full Name: Dr. Hugo Strange

Occupation: Psychiatrist, school counselor, criminal

Height: 5ft 10½in

Weight: 170 lbs

Base: Gotham City

Allies: Eli Strange, Crazy Quilt, Dr. Death

Foes: Batman, the Batman Family

POWERS AND ABILITIES

Extremely persuasive and manipulative; expert scientist known for his unorthodox experiments; well connected in the criminal underground and Super Hero community; highly intelligent; in excellent physical condition.

THE DOCTOR IS IN

A bit of a psychiatrist to the stars when not plotting the downfall of Batman, Hugo Strange has been known to give personal counsel to Arsenal, Red Hood's partner and longtime Outlaws teammate.

It has been difficult for Batman to prove the corrupt nature of Professor Hugo Strange. Despite their frequent clashes, Hugo keeps reemerging in the Dark Knight's life in various legitimate positions. One of the infamous Doctors Three alongside Crazy Quilt and Dr. Death, Hugo is now a counselor at Gotham Academy, as if his past crimes never occurred.

"I'll keep our talks a secret. I am here to help you."

Strange takes pride in manipulating the minds of others for his own selfish gain, especially the aspiring young students at Gotham Academy.

ROGUE

VITAL STATS

Full Name: Victor Zsasz

Occupation: Criminal

Height: 5ft 8in

Weight: 150 lbs

Base: Gotham City

Ally: Emperor Blackgate

Foes: Batman, the Penguin, Merrymaker

POWERS AND ABILITIES

Deadly efficient murderer; excellent physical condition; mentally unstable and obsessed with murder; usually prefers using blades or knives.

DEATH TALLY

One of Gotham City's most dangerous and psychotic villains, Mr. Zsasz likes to keep a tally of his kills. For every person he murders, he carves a notch in his own flesh to remember them by.

Victor Zsasz has an addictive personality, and was therefore an easy mark when he gambled in the Penguin's Iceberg Casino. The heir to Zsasz Industries, Victor lost all his money thanks to the Penguin encouraging his love of gambling. Victor's mind snapped, and he embarked on a killing spree that continues to this day, despite Batman's efforts to stop him.

"The bird-man. This was all his doing. He gave me the knife."

While he usually prefers to work alone, Zsasz has been the willing pawn of Emperor Blackgate in the past, helping to spread the Man-Bat virus.

THE CRIME SYNDICATE

VITAL STATS

Group Name: The Crime Syndicate

Base: Happy Harbor, Rhode Island

Allies: The Secret Society

Foes: The Justice League, Mazahs, Lex Luthor, the Justice League of America

Members:
Owlman, Ultraman, Superwoman, Power Ring (deceased), Johnny Quick (deceased), Atomica (deceased), Sea King (deceased), Deathstorm (deceased), Grid (deceased)

INJUSTICE FOR ALL

The Crime Syndicate are the evil equivalent of the Justice League, headed by three notorious super-villains: Ultraman is the dark mirror to Superman; Superwoman is the corrupted version of Wonder Woman, and Owlman is Earth-Three's evil Batman.

In the parallel dimension of Earth-Three, evil overshadows good. There, the Crime Syndicate served as an evil Justice League of sorts. When the Crime Syndicate fled to the Justice League's dimension, they banished the Justice League to a prison inside the matrix of the hero Firestorm. Meanwhile, they caused a planet-wide blackout and declared themselves rulers of the world.

"This world is ours."

Despite uniting the world's super-villains, the Crime Syndicate finally fell when Batman and a team of villains invaded the Syndicate's headquarters.

SIGNALMAN

VITAL STATS

Real Name: Phil Cobb
Occupation: Criminal
Height: 6ft 2in
Weight: 200 lbs
Base: Gotham City
Allies: Blockbuster, the
Secret Society, Firefly,
Cluemaster, Lock-Up
Foes: Batman, the
Batman Family

POWERS AND ABILITIES

Employs a variety of
signal-themed gadgets;
very intelligent, with strong
computer hacking skills;
keeps himself in excellent
physical condition;
cultivates connections
with many minor criminals.

ANSWERING THE SIGNAL

The Signalman seems to
join any club that will have
him as a member, so it
made complete sense when
he was an early supporter
of the villain Outsider and
a member of the nefarious
Secret Society.

Small-time criminal Phil Cobb
decided to up his game when he
reached Gotham City after seeing the
Bat-Signal shining over the skyline.
He opted for the identity of Signalman,
and his sign-themed robberies soon
drew Batman's attention. Involved in
Cluemaster and Lincoln March's plan
to kill the Dark Knight, he also played
a major role in the Secret Society.

*"In this town, you learn not
to assume anything."*

One of Signalman's greatest strengths is
his ability to hack into a city's traffic system,
controlling the traffic lights as he sees fit.

BLOCKBUSTER

ROGUE

VITAL STATS

Real Name: Mark Desmond
Occupation: Criminal
Height: 8ft
Weight: 825 lbs
Base: Gotham City
Allies: The Secret Society,
the Fist of Cain, Roland
Desmond
Foes: Batman, Hawkman,
the Batman Family,
Superman

POWERS AND ABILITIES

Superhuman strength,
durability, and endurance;
almost completely incapable of
thought; prone to fits of rage.

BATTLE OF THE BLOCKBUSTERS

When Blockbuster returned to his
enormous form, he fought another
transformed patient, Professor
Ziegler. However, after defeat
at Blockbuster's hands, Ziegler
returned to his normal human state.

Chemist Mark Desmond was working
on a treatment that would stop violent
behavior. However, he was accidentally
transformed into a raging behemoth
called Blockbuster. After battles with
Batman, Robin, and Superman, he found
himself at the Rest Haven medical facility
—human again and being treated for
dementia. But soon, steroid treatments
restored his monstrous Blockbuster form.

*"I am Blockbuster—
and I crush all!"*

Blockbuster later joined the infamous Secret
Society where his brute strength is a powerful
weapon in the clandestine group's arsenal.

DARKSEID

VITAL STATS

Real Name: Uxas

Occupation: Ruler of Apokolips

Height: 8ft 9in

Weight: 1,815 lbs

Base: Apokolips

Allies: Desaad, Kalibak, Granny Goodness, Parademons

Foes: The Justice League, Batman, Superman, Highfather, Orion

POWERS AND ABILITIES

Omega Effect eye beams can kill, resurrect, harm, or send victims hurtling through time; superhuman strength and endurance; commands armies of Parademons, elite soldiers, and a planet of minions.

GOD AMONG MEN

Darkseid had conquered many worlds before, including Earth-Two, a parallel dimension to the Earth of the Justice League. So when the League chased him off their planet, he swore revenge.

The planet Apokolips has been at war with its neighboring world New Genesis for years. Darkseid is the ruler of Apokolips and wants nothing less than to achieve mastery over death and rule the universe. To that end, he has clashed with the Justice League and Batman, when the Dark Knight traveled to Apokolips to rescue the body of the temporarily dead Damian Wayne.

Eyes produce devastating Omega Beams

Stone-like body can overpower even Superman

Towers over members of the Justice League

"You came a long way to die."

131

SUICIDE SQUAD

VITAL STATS

Team Name: Task Force X, Suicide Squad

Base: Belle Reve Penitentiary

Allies: Amanda Waller, Vic Sage, James Gordon, Jr.

Foes: Deathstroke, Basilisk, The League

Members: Deadshot, Harley Quinn, Captain Boomerang, Reverse-Flash, Parasite, Black Manta, King Shark (former), the Joker's Daughter (former), Cheetah (former), Savant (former), Unknown Soldier (former), Iceberg (former), Crowbar (former), El Diablo (former), Light (former), Lime (deceased), Voltaic (deceased), Yo-Yo (deceased), Black Spider (traitor), Deathstroke (traitor)

DEADLY DISAGREEMENTS
Keeping the Squad in line during missions often proves difficult. The Joker's Daughter and Harley Quinn don't see eye to eye and Deathstroke betrayed the team to the Russians.

Task Force X is a secret team, run by Amanda Waller for the US government. Made up of convicted criminals in super-villain costumes, the task force cannot be linked to the government. The roster constantly changes, as different criminals are chosen for their particular sets of skills. The team's nickname—Suicide Squad—reflects the deadly nature of its missions.

"I want to use prisoners with nothing to lose and everything to gain."

The Squad is kept in line by explosives implanted at the base of their necks. If they try to escape or change the mission, Waller can detonate them.

ROGUE

VITAL STATS

Real Name: Floyd Lawton

Occupation: Mercenary

Height: 6ft 1in

Weight: 193 lbs

Base: Belle Reve Penitentiary

Allies: Suicide Squad, Amanda Waller, Harley Quinn

Foes: Batman, Deathstroke

POWERS AND ABILITIES

One of the best marksmen on the planet; armed with wrist cannons and an eye sight in his mask; wears armored suit; adept at using nearly all types of firearms; efficient hand-to-hand combatant; eyesight can see various light spectrums.

FIRING SQUAD

As a member of the Suicide Squad, it seems as though Deadshot has found purpose in his life. He views some people—like his boss Amanda Waller—as a gun, and himself as a bullet, waiting to be fired.

Floyd Lawton was a poor boy growing up in the slums of Gotham City. One day, bullets from a nearby shooting came through the wall of his home and killed his family. That day, Lawton swore revenge and taught himself to shoot. He finally found and shot the men responsible, later finding employment with their boss as a sharpshooter.

Helmet protects against enemy fire

Loves guns, large and small

Eye sight synced with wrist guns

Carries weapons and plenty of ammunition

"I never miss."

DEATHSTROKE

CLASHING WITH DEATH

A gun for hire, Deathstroke is billed as one of the world's best assassins. He has fought many fearsome opponents, from Batman and Harley Quinn to Wonder Woman and Lobo, managing to survive every fight.

Young Slade Wilson lied about his age in order to enlist in the army when he was only 16. He advanced quickly through the ranks, and soon joined the special ops group, Team 7. Slade was later the subject of a government experiment that made him into a super-soldier. He began life as an assassin and mercenary for hire: Deathstroke, the Terminator.

"Smiling? You like pain, Batman?"

Prefers to use swords and firearms

Talented marksman

Wears armored suit in combat

Has worn several costumes over the years

Carries multiple weapons at all times

CALENDAR MAN

ROGUE

VITAL STATS

Real Name: Julian Day
Occupation: Criminal
Height: 6ft 11in
Weight: 290 lbs
Base: Gotham City
Ally: The Squid
Foe: Batman

POWERS AND ABILITIES

Bulky and muscular; experienced brawler; obsessed with holidays, days of the week, and the calendar.

MARKING THE CALENDAR

When Batman met Aden Day, the boy was not being treated well. Batman donned his often-used criminal disguise as "Matches" Malone, and hit Julian Day's head against some tiles, creating a calendar-like scar on the villain's face.

Scarred face resembles a calendar

Extremely strong and muscular

Julian Day was a single father with a young son, Aden. In order to make ends meet, he took work as a hired thug for the crime boss known as the Squid. Julian was an excellent enforcer, but he was a terrible father. When Batman learned that Aden was not being looked after well enough, he confronted Julian and placed Aden in a good home.

"Calendar...get... a...calendar..."

CATMAN

VITAL STATS

Real Name: Thomas Blake
Occupation: Bounty hunter
Height: 6ft
Weight: 179 lbs
Base: Gotham City
Allies: The Secret Six
Foes: Batman, the Riddler

POWERS AND ABILITIES

Expert hand-to-hand combatant; feels oneness with big cats and is never harmed by them; handsome, with natural charisma and animal magnetism; extremely fit and agile; excellent senses; ferocious temperament.

FELINE SENSES

Once, Catman was simply minding his own business at a bar in New Mexico when he was kidnapped by the Riddler's men. Despite his captors telling him they worked for the Bureau of Alcohol, Tobacco, and Firearms, Catman sniffed them out as imposters.

A bounty hunter who was kidnapped by the Riddler, Thomas Blake was held captive with only a pet kitten to keep him sane. After a year, he was set free until he was captured again, this time with five other criminals: the Riddler had a vendetta against the six for ruining the night of his marriage proposal. However, Blake and the others escaped, forming the Secret Six.

"We're not the good guys."

Catman befriended Secret Six member, Big Shot, not realizing that Big Shot was Ralph Dibny, a man taking orders from the Six's enemy, the Riddler.

CAVALIER

VITAL STATS

Real Name: Mortimer Drake
Occupation: Criminal
Height: 6ft 1in
Weight: 182 lbs
Base: Gotham City
Allies: Arkham Asylum Inmates
Foes: Batman, the Batman Family, Batwoman

POWERS AND ABILITIES

Expert swordsman known to use electrified rapier; proficient with firearms; witty; adept strategist; costume armed with unexpected weapons; adept hand-to-hand combatant.

ESCAPE ARTIST
Despite being defeated by the Dark Knight on several occasions, Cavalier is quick to raise his rapier against Batman given the chance, participating in two recent Arkham Asylum breakouts.

An early foe of Batman's, Mortimer Drake adopted the name and mantle of the Cavalier after his love of antiques inspired him to rob museums for the finest collectibles known to man. Despite being confined to Arkham Asylum by Batman, Cavalier escaped during a breakout, but luckily, Batwoman was on hand to take the villain down yet again.

"Methinks a palpable and bloody hit—"

Smiles in the face of adversity

Often openly challenges Batman to a duel

Costume similar to those of the Three Musketeers

CRAZY QUILT

VITAL STATS

Real Name: Dr. Paul Dekker

Occupation: Scientist

Height: 5ft 11in

Weight: 172 lbs

Base: Gotham City

Allies: Philip Kane, Dr. Death, Hugo Strange, the Joker

Foe: Batman

POWERS AND ABILITIES

Unparalleled genius who created a way for cells to become new again; severely mentally unhinged; extremely knowledgeable in history; obsessed with the chemical compound Dionesium; carries and uses a firearm.

A STITCH IN CRIME

Paul Dekker was born in the Narrows to a poor family of artists who perished due to a broken gas pipe. A genius, Dekker invented an amazing medical process called "the healing stitch," but his mind later slipped into insanity.

When Bruce Wayne's uncle, Philip Kane, ran Wayne Enterprises, he hired the notorious Doctors Three: Dr. Karl Helfern, who worked in bone; Professor Hugo Strange, neural matter expert; and Dr. Paul Dekker, who worked in soft tissue. Like his partners, Dekker's life deteriorated, and he became an Arkham Asylum inmate after doing terrible things in order to meet Batman.

"Doesn't feel like a Batman story anymore, does it?"

Crazy Quilt used his incredible scientific skills to help the Joker develop a virus, which the Joker later released on Gotham City.

CLUEMASTER

VITAL STATS

Real Name: Arthur Brown

Occupation: Criminal, former game show host

Height: 5ft 11in

Weight: 169 lbs

Base: Gotham City

Allies: Lock-Up, Signalman, Firefly, Lincoln March

Foes: Spoiler, Batman, the Batman Family

POWERS AND ABILITIES

Clever strategist; trivia expert obsessed with clues; wears protective suit and hi-tech goggles; armed with weaponized capsules called plasti-pellets; connections to powerful figures in Gotham City underworld.

CLUELESS

Teaming with Lincoln March and several supposedly "D-list" villains, Cluemaster set out to rid Gotham City of Batman. Unfortunately, he didn't count on his own daughter, Spoiler, discovering one of his late night meetings with his accomplices.

The host of "Quizbowl," a trivia game show, Arthur Brown lost his job after yelling at a contestant. Upset that the "intellectually inferior" were wealthy while he was poor, he embarked on a life of crime as the Cluemaster. He attempted to prove his superiority over his robbery victims by leaving clues behind, clues that eventually led to his capture by Batman.

"I have taken everything from you, piece by piece."

Cluemaster used his ability to fly under the radar and plot the near-death of Batman, until he was seemingly killed by Lincoln March.

PARAGON

VITAL STATS

Real Name: Unknown

Occupation: Criminal cult leader

Height: 6ft

Weight: 194 lbs

Base: Gotham City

Allies: Republic of Tomorrow

Foes: Dick Grayson, G.C.P.D.

POWERS AND ABILITIES
Expert at use of duel energy blades with rotating plasma core; leads cult of similarly armored and weaponized extremists; genius-level intellect and thermodynamics expert; keen manipulator.

HERE TODAY, PARAGON TOMORROW
Nightwing discovered that Paragon had framed him for the murder of two of the Republic of Tomorrow's members. He confronted the villain and eventually turned him over to police custody.

Paragon is the leader of a fanatical cult known as the Republic of Tomorrow. As a teenager, he studied thermodynamics and was able to build a working reactor at just 16 years old. After developing a rotating plasma core to power energy blades, he adopted the name Paragon and began leading a group of armed cultists into what he viewed as a better tomorrow.

"The revolution, Nightwing... begins with your death!"

Enhanced sight through lenses

Wears armored body suit

Paragon's symbol, worn by all followers

Designed energy blades himself

PRANKSTER

VITAL STATS

Real Name: Oswald Loomis
Occupation: Criminal
Height: 5ft 10in
Weight: 170 lbs
Base: Chicago
Ally: Cluemaster
Foes: Dick Grayson, Mayor
Wallace Cole, Batman

POWERS AND ABILITIES

Genius-level computer
hacker; master manipulator
with dozens of followers;
access to funds that allow
for elaborate death traps;
cunning, with a mind
for revenge.

PULLING THE PRANK

When temporarily living in
Chicago, Nightwing took on
the Prankster and narrowly
avoided dying in the villain's
death traps. The Prankster
was later defeated by Tony
Zucco, the man who killed
Nightwing's parents.

Loves to
play cunning
mind games

Mask similar
to his childhood
costume

When Oswald Loomis was a boy,
his father was killed on Halloween
night—a crime for which the criminal
William Cole was jailed. Loomis was
wearing a Halloween mask that night,
which he mailed to Cole, as a promise
of revenge. He eventually got his
payback when he framed William
Cole's brother, Wallace, the mayor
of Chicago, for embezzlement.

"...where's the prank?"

AMYGDALA

ROGUE

VITAL STATS

Real Name: Aaron Helzinger

Occupation: Criminal

Height: 7ft 5in

Weight: 343 lbs

Base: Gotham City

Ally: Knightfall

Foes: Dick Grayson, Batman, Batgirl

POWERS AND ABILITIES

Near superhuman strength, endurance, speed, and durability; almost mindless, with an uncontrollable berserker rage.

RIOT ON THE STREETS

Confused and easily disorientated, Amygdala was once hired by the villain Knightfall to cause havoc on Gotham City's streets alongside other villains including the Mad Hatter, Clayface, and Mr. Zsasz.

During the infamous Gotham City blackout, a mentally unstable behemoth of a man named Aaron Helzinger was undergoing brain surgery. Waking on the operating table—and lacking his brain's rage-controlling amygdala—he smashed his way out of the hospital and began to rampage through the streets. He chanced upon a young Dick Grayson and earned his nickname, Amygdala.

"...it hurtssssss!"

Grayson and his friends and performers at Haly's Circus escaped Amygdala's clutches, subduing the monster when he fell from a rooftop ledge.

THE RED HOOD GANG

VITAL STATS

Team Name: The Red Hood Gang

Base: Gotham City

Allies: Fellow Red Hood members

Foes: Batman, G.C.P.D., the Penguin, the Falcone Family

Members:
Red Hood One (possibly the Joker), the original Red Hood One (Liam Distal), Philip Kane, dozens of mysterious members

A PLAGUE ON GOTHAM CITY
The citizens of Gotham City lived in fear during the Red Hood Gang's reign of terror. The well-dressed thugs robbed banks, destroyed buildings, and made the city streets unsafe. Most people were too afraid to stand up to the violent gang—but not Bruce Wayne.

When Bruce Wayne returned home from training abroad, Gotham City was plagued by the Red Hood Gang. Led by the notorious Red Hood One, the gang was taking over some of the Falcone gang's territory. Before he adopted his identity as Batman, Bruce opposed the gang, only to have them destroy his operations base near Crime Alley, almost killing him in the process.

"Gotham's Finest! Kill them all!"

After Bruce was injured by the Red Hood Gang, he realized he had to become more than a man to take them on—and so his Batman persona was born.

ANARKY

VITAL STATS

Real Name: Sam Young

Occupation: Criminal anarchist

Height: 6ft 2in

Weight: 215 lbs

Base: Gotham City

Allies: Cult of followers

Foes: Batman, the Mad Hatter, Harvey Bullock

POWERS AND ABILITIES

Natural leader and extremely manipulative; highly intelligent; commands a cult-like army of devoted followers; many connections in the political world.

FOR THE PEOPLE?

Although he was later proven a fraud by the combined efforts of Batman and Harvey Bullock, Anarky managed to inspire many people during his crusade, including a young man named Lonnie Machin.

When Anarky emerged in Gotham City, he brought with him a revolution. However, it was all smoke and mirrors. When Sam Young was a child, his sister was killed by the Mad Hatter. Wanting revenge, Young adopted the identity of Anarky and killed the Hatter's old cohort under cover of the fake rebellion. Batman stopped the villain before he could kill the Hatter.

"Shape your own future. The Anarky revolution begins today."

Anarky handed out thousands of masks based on his sister's face, and encouraged Gotham City's citizens to start their lives anew.

MIRROR

VITAL STATS

Real Name: Jonathan Mills

Occupation: Criminal, former federal agent

Height: 6ft

Weight: 205 lbs

Base: Gotham City

Allies: Knightfall, Grotesque, Gretel

Foes: Batgirl, James Gordon

POWERS AND ABILITIES

Highly skilled fighter; extremely athletic; trained former federal agent; expert marksman; protective suit includes spiked knuckles and Utility Belt equipped with weapons and small gadgets.

TWISTED REFLECTION

Mirror keeps a list of individuals he believes should have died, and does his best to remedy that "oversight." One such name was James Gordon, before Batgirl interfered and saved her father's life.

Federal agent Jonathan Mills was the only survivor of a car crash that took the lives of his wife and twin daughters. He felt he had been fated to die, and decided to dedicate his life to killing others whom he believed should not have survived their near death experiences. After clashing with Batgirl, he later went to work for the criminal Knightfall.

"And you're not on the list."

Mirror was one of the first villains Batgirl fought after returning to life as a vigilante. So naturally, she was a bit nervous when facing him.

ARCHITECT

ROGUE

VITAL STATS

Real Name: Dillon May

Occupation: Criminal

Height: 6ft

Weight: 197 lbs

Base: Gotham City

Allies: Hush, Nicholas and Bradley Gates

Foes: Batman, the Batman Family

POWERS AND ABILITIES

Modified construction suit grants him durability, speed, enhanced strength, and endurance; suit's limited oxygen supply allows for periods of underwater activity; mentally unbalanced with a serious vendetta against Gotham City's most powerful families.

GATES OF GOTHAM CITY

When Dillon May adopted the suit of the Architect, he had no idea he was basing his vendetta on the words of a madman. Extended suit use leads to severe decompression sickness, and caused Dillon to lose his grip on reality.

In the late 1800s, Nicholas and Bradley Gates helped construct most of Gotham City's important buildings. Bradley made an underwater suit, but when he was murdered, Nicholas put on the suit to kill the likely culprit. Decades later, Gates's descendant, Dillon May, donned the suit, called himself the Architect, and began destroying Gotham City's historical buildings.

Oxygen reserve allows for underwater use

Costume retains its 1800's steampunk style

Hydraulics increase wearer's speed

"...I wonder if you might come out and play?"

DR. PHOSPHORUS

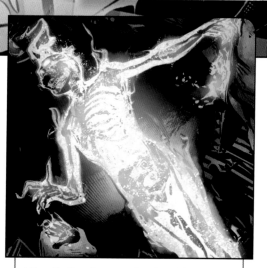

VITAL STATS

Real Name: Alexander Sartorius

Occupation: Criminal, underground tribe leader

Height: 5ft 11in

Weight: 169 lbs

Base: Gotham City

Allies: Deacon Blackfire, Tinderbox

Foes: Batman, Catwoman, the Joker's Daughter

POWERS AND ABILITIES

Can shoot radioactive phosphorus flame at enemies; burns constantly with poisonous fumes; brilliant mind and natural leader; commands army of underground citizens.

RING OF FIRE

When clashing with Catwoman and the Joker's Daughter in the Gotham City underground, Dr. Phosphorus revealed that his ultimate desire was to turn Gotham City into a giant volcano by causing explosions in the underground.

Catwoman first stumbled across Dr. Phosphorus when she was searching for her friend Rat-Tail in the vast passageways under Gotham City. She passed into Charneltown, the area that Phosphorus ruled with his daughter, Tinderbox. Phosphorus revealed that he had been the victim of a nuclear accident and had fled to Charneltown so he could live somewhere hot.

"...I could flick my finger and fry you to a cinder."

When Dr. Phosphorus was imprisoned in Arkham Asylum, doctors summoned some of the country's top scientists to work out how to stop him from burning.

THE CREEPER

VITAL STATS

Real Name: Jack Ryder

Occupation: Criminal, former reporter

Height: 6ft

Weight: 194 lbs

Base: Mobile

Ally: Killer Croc

Foes: Katana, Batman

POWERS AND ABILITIES

Hosts a mystical demon; superhuman strength, agility, endurance, and durability; able to leap far distances; carries chains that he uses as weapons; can create manufactured tornadoes with his chains.

CREEPING THROUGH

The Oni Demon known as the Creeper came to our reality through a "crack in the world" during 16th century Japan. Twenty years later, he was discovered and imprisoned in the magical Soultaker sword.

Jack Ryder, a famous TV personality, was killed while reporting on a giant monster. Meanwhile, the Super Hero Katana was locked in battle with Killer Croc, who shattered her Soultaker sword, freeing a demon called the Creeper. These seemingly unrelated events converged when the Creeper took possession of Ryder's body, resurrecting Jack in the process.

"The Creeper rides again."

When Katana pieced her Soultaker sword back together, the Creeper became one of the main targets on her list.

ROGUE

VITAL STATS

Real Name: Unknown

Occupation: Arkham Asylum inmate

Height: 5ft 2in

Weight: 84 lbs

Base: Gotham City

Allies: Dr. Jeremiah Arkham, Dr. Amadeus Arkham

Foes: Batman, the Joker's Daughter

POWERS AND ABILITIES

Has the ability to "quantum tunnel," or walk through walls; able to toy with the minds and memories of her victims; able to alter her own appearance.

BLAMING THE BAT

The Anchoress wrongly blames Batman for turning Arkham Asylum into a terrible place, rather than the peaceful asylum it used to be before the emergence of villains like the Joker and Mr. Zsasz.

Born sometime before the 1900s, the woman who would become the Anchoress was interested in physics. When her parents tried to marry her off, a struggle ensued, ending with the Anchoress being knocked into a shelf full of chemicals. The resulting explosion killed her parents and gave her new abilities that enabled her to project her body's energy through various objects.

"They've all forgotten me here..."

Appears helpless and frail

Can alter her appearance

Can enter one's mind with a touch

REAPER

VITAL STATS

Real Name: Dr. Benjamin Gruener

Occupation: Criminal

Height: 5ft 10in

Weight: 166 lbs

Base: Gotham City

Allies: Bane, Blackgate Penitentiary Inmates

Foes: Batman, the Falcone Family, Sumo, Firefly

POWERS AND ABILITIES

Wears armored suit that strikes fear into those who encounter it; well-versed in medicine; adept hand-to-hand fighter; gauntlets contain sickle blades and firearms.

FLOWERS AT THE GRAVE

Batman recently battled the Reaper in the back of a floral truck with the help of Robin. The Reaper was attempting to send poisonous flowers to a wake for a member of the Falcone family.

Benjamin Gruener grew up in Germany during World War II, and was a survivor of the holocaust. He became a medical doctor, but his past made him fixate on revenge and he lost his sanity. As the Reaper, he has mysteriously cheated death to seek deadly justice for Gotham City's criminals, although he often clashes with the metropolis's true champion, the Batman.

"Now it's time to die."

After a riot in Blackgate Penitentiary instigated by Bane's forces, the Reaper joined Bane in a fight against the Arkham Asylum inmates.

VITAL STATS

Team Name: The Club of Villains

Base: Gotham City

Allies: The Black Glove

Foes: Batman, the Batman Family, the Club of Heroes

Members: Dr. Simon Hurt, Charlie Caligula, Scorpiana, El Sombrero, Le Bossu, Swagman, King Kraken, Pierrot Lunaire

THE CLUB SCENE
When Dr. Hurt attacked Batman directly, the rest of the Club of Villains attacked Batman's allies. However, the Club of Heroes arrived in Gotham City to even the odds and give Batman time to triumph over the Black Glove.

Dr. Hurt waited decades to take over Gotham City, and had meanwhile formed many alliances with nefarious groups, including the Club of Villains. Created as the counterpart to Batman's allies in the Club of Heroes, the villains hailed from all over the globe. Many of them had clashed with Club of Heroes members, such as El Gaucho. The Club was a small part of Hurt's larger conspiracy, the Black Glove.

"Come, take your place for the danse macabre."

Batman gained a whole new Rogues Gallery when Dr. Hurt assembled his Club of Villains, and many of the villains have gone on to challenge Batman, Inc.

VITAL STATS

Real Name: Dr. Karl Helfern
Occupation: Former scientist
Height: Varies with mutations
Weight: Varies with mutations
Base: Gotham City
Allies: The Riddler, Crazy Quilt, Dr. Hugo Strange
Foes: Batman, Poison Ivy, James Gordon, Lucius Fox

POWERS AND ABILITIES

Superhuman strength, endurance, and durability; armed with serum that causes rapid bone growth to the point of death; brilliant scientist; body constantly healing in strange new bone formations.

DEATH COMES KNOCKING

After becoming unstable and losing his job at Wayne Enterprises, Dr. Death injected himself with an experimental bone-hardening formula, adopting a monstrous form. He used his new abilities to kill his former colleagues, under the Riddler's employ.

Years ago, during a citywide blackout, the police discovered a series of grotesque murder victims. The culprit was Dr. Death, a mysterious man who earned his nickname by experimenting on animals in illegal labs. After looking into Dr. Death's past, Batman battled the villain above Gotham City, a fight that Death seemingly didn't survive.

"I've been waiting so long to meet you, after all."

Brilliant mind bent on revenge

Serum causes elongated proportions

Teeth grown into disturbing fangs

JACKANAPES

ROGUE

VITAL STATS

Real Name: Jackanapes
Occupation: Criminal
Height: 7ft 3in
Weight: 453 lbs
Base: Gotham City
Ally: The Joker
Foes: Batman, the
Batman Family

POWERS AND ABILITIES

Typical strength, stamina,
and endurance of a large
gorilla; quick learner.

FUTURE THREAT
According to the Joker, Jackanapes was
a fast learner and could even work on
intricate machinery. If true, this intelligent
gorilla could prove to be a major foe of
Batman in the future.

One day, at Gotham County Zoo,
the Joker spotted a baby gorilla
playing with a stuffed monkey toy,
similar to one he had as a child.
The Joker kidnapped the gorilla and
began to raise it as his own, training
it in the ways of murder. However,
Jackanapes seemingly died when he
was knocked off a blimp during one
of the Joker's elaborate crimes.

"..."

Trained in
operating
firearms

Jester costume
complements
the Joker's

Armed with
deadly weapons
at all times

JAMES GORDON, JR.

VITAL STATS

Full Name: James Gordon, Jr.
Occupation: Criminal
Height: 5ft 10in
Weight: 159 lbs
Base: Gotham City
Allies: Knightfall, Suicide Squad
Foes: Batgirl, James Gordon, Barbara Kean Gordon

POWERS AND ABILITIES

Psychotic master plotter and manipulator; many underworld connections; extremely intelligent; expert at covering up his crimes; aware of Batgirl's double life.

KILLER INSTINCT

When James Gordon, Jr. reemerged in Batgirl's life, he played twisted games with his sister, even attempting to kill their mother, Barbara Kean Gordon. During one dramatic fight, Batgirl defeated James, mistakenly believing she'd killed him.

As a baby, James Gordon, Jr. never cried, and as he got older, his family could sense coldness behind his eyes. When James killed the family cat and threatened the same violence to his sister Barbara, his mother left, abandoning Barbara in the process. Barbara grew up to become Batgirl, while James grew up to be every bit as evil as his family knew him to be.

"You. Will. Never. Be free of me."

James knows Barbara Gordon well enough to manipulate her. He even let Batgirl believe he was dead while he served as a Suicide Squad advisor.

BLACK MASK

VITAL STATS

Real Name: Roman Sionis

Occupation: Criminal

Height: 6ft 1in

Weight: 195 lbs

Base: Gotham City

Allies: The False Face Society

Foes: Batman, the Mad Hatter

POWERS AND ABILITIES

Wears ebony mask that seems to give him telepathic and telekinetic powers; natural leader; expert strategist; capable hand-to-hand combatant; very intelligent; expert in torture techniques.

MASK VS. HAT

Black Mask's father's casket has long been one of the holy grails for the Mad Hatter, another of Batman's foes obsessed with mind control. This put the Hatter and Black Mask at odds, and made them natural rivals.

The rich yet disturbed heir to the Janus Cosmetics company, Roman Sionis was rumored to have played an active part in his parents' death when their home burned to the ground. Obsessed with masks, Roman carved his infamous black mask out of his father's coffin, later discovering that the casket was made of a strange material that gave him special abilities.

"Can't you see your mind is too weak to defend against my probe?!"

Uses mask to control False Face Society

Accustomed to wearing expensive clothe[s]

Fancy suit juxtaposed with frightful mask terrifies foes

BLACK SPIDER

EYE OF THE SPIDER
Black Spider's mask is equipped with special lenses that allow him to utilize thermal imaging and get a better read on his target, even in a room that's pitch black or obscured by smoke.

VITAL STATS

Real Name: Eric Needham

Occupation: Vigilante

Height: 5ft 10in

Weight: 173 lbs

Base: Gotham City

Ally: Basilisk

Foes: Batman, Suicide Squad, Amanda Waller

POWERS AND ABILITIES
Master martial artist; wears armored suit equipped with a variety of weapons and devices; weapons expert who often uses kamas; excellent athlete and gymnast; strong desire to seek vengeance against all criminals.

When government agent Amanda Waller proposed the idea of the Suicide Squad, a task force of super-villains that offered her complete deniability, Black Spider was a top choice on her list of recruits. An old enemy of Batman, Black Spider was a Gotham City vigilante whose violent methods proved too extreme for the Dark Knight.

"I'm not done here yet."

While on the Suicide Squad, Black Spider proved he was as corrupt as ever when he betrayed the team to the terrorist organization called Basilisk.

MAXIE ZEUS

VITAL STATS

Full Name: Maximilian Zeus

Occupation: Criminal

Height: 5ft 6in

Weight: 135 lbs

Base: Gotham City

Allies: Deacon Blackfire, Professor Milo, the Joker's Daughter

Foes: Batman, Batwing, the Batman Family

POWERS AND ABILITIES

Fit and athletic; capable hand-to-hand combatant; intelligent natural leader with a severe god complex; many connections in the business world and the criminal underworld.

THE POWER OF ZEUS

While staying in Arkham Asylum, Maxie Zeus was rendered near catatonic and felt nothing. This made him especially difficult to best in a fight, as the hero Batwing soon discovered firsthand.

For a time, Maxie Zeus was a successful crime boss in Gotham City. However, he began to lose his grip on reality and think of himself as a god, despite being bested by his enemy, the Batman. Later sentenced to a stay in Arkham Asylum, Zeus briefly hosted the spirit of Deacon Blackfire in his own body. This led to a battle with Batwing and the Spectre.

*"Bow down **to me**, mortal."*

Zeus was treated like the god he believed he was when he joined a cult intent on resurrecting Deacon Blackfire, whose spirit possessed his body.

EMPEROR BLACKGATE

VITAL STATS

Real Name: Ignatius Ogilvy

Occupation: Criminal

Height: 6ft 3in

Weight: 225 lbs

Base: Gotham City

Allies: Poison Ivy,
Mr. Mosaic, Hypnotic,
Imperceptible Man,
Mr. Zsasz

Foes: Batman, the Penguin,
the Batman Family

POWERS AND ABILITIES

Brilliant strategist who
quickly climbed the criminal
ranks; superhuman
strength and durability
from serum partially
created by Poison Ivy.

KING OF THE MOUNTAIN

After powering himself
up with a combination
of Man-Bat serum,
Venom, and a plant-
based formula,
Emperor Penguin was
arrested and taken to
jail. There he quickly
became the so-called
king of the prison,
changing his moniker
to Emperor Blackgate.

Unafraid to steal
the Penguin's
fashion and title

Master
manipulator
with high IQ

Powerful
connections in
the underworld

Ignatius Ogilvy rose to power as the
Penguin's right hand man. But when
the Joker forced the Penguin to help
him in his latest scheme, Ogilvy
claimed the Penguin's empire for
his own as Emperor Penguin. He
injected himself with a secret formula
to become a physical threat, but was
ultimately defeated by Batman and
incarcerated in Blackgate Penitentiary.

*"The dawn of a new era...and the
empire of Emperor Penguin."*

FIREBUG

ROGUE

VITAL STATS

Real Name: Unknown

Occupation: Criminal, arsonist

Height: 5ft 9in

Weight: 180 lbs

Base: Gotham City

Allies: Various employers

Foes: Batgirl, Batman

POWERS AND ABILITIES

Uses military grade fast-burning accelerant to start and spread fires; wears protective fireproof armor; employs rocket launchers and incendiary grenades; single-minded focus on his mission once hired.

SOLDIER OF FORTUNE?

Little is known about Firebug's past, but the medals he wears on his otherwise unadorned suit imply a military background. He is obviously highly skilled, and shows no signs of guilt or remorse for his actions.

While probably not as well known as the similar Gotham City villain, Firefly, Firebug doesn't let the competition get to him. As a freelance arsonist, Firebug takes his jobs seriously, recently clashing with Batgirl when she was tracking down accomplices of the Joker. Killing police officers at the behest of his employer, Firebug was eventually defeated by the determined Batgirl.

"You shouldn't have come here to mess with Firebug, girl!"

Firebug's suit seems more utilitarian than those of most costumed criminals. A consummate professional, he prides himself on his work.

FIREFLY

ROGUE

VITAL STATS

Real Name: Ted Carson

Occupation: Criminal

Height: 5ft 11in

Weight: 167 lbs

Base: Gotham City

Allies: Cluemaster, Lock-Up, Signalman

Foes: Batman, Dick Grayson, Batgirl, the Batman Family

POWERS AND ABILITIES

Uses stolen Firefly suit that is capable of flight and protects wearer from heat and other damage; suit can fire blasts of flame; equipped with flame sword and incendiary grenades.

FLY VS. FLY

Ted Carson stole technology and the name Firefly from Garfield Lynns, a talented, yet easily angered pyrotechnics expert. His advanced Firefly suit can fly with the use of fiery wings.

Movie star **Cindy Cooke** had lots of adoring and obsessive fans. So when her talent agency, production company, and the home of her ex-boyfriend, Ted Carson, burned down, there were plenty of suspects. It took the combined efforts of Nightwing and Batgirl to discover that Carson himself was the Firefly, having faked his own death in order to live a private life with Cindy.

> *"I'm sorry...but this is personal."*

As Firefly, Carson attempted to frame the deceased Garfield Lynns for his crimes, but all his attacks were merely an elaborate smokescreen.

PROFESSOR MILO

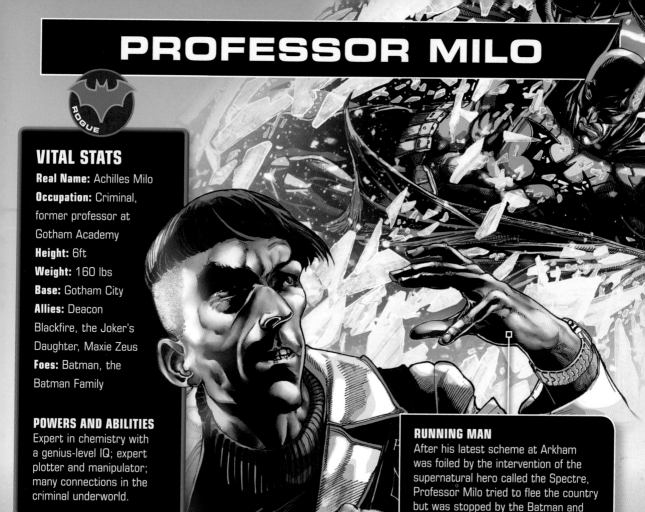

ROGUE

VITAL STATS

Real Name: Achilles Milo

Occupation: Criminal, former professor at Gotham Academy

Height: 6ft

Weight: 160 lbs

Base: Gotham City

Allies: Deacon Blackfire, the Joker's Daughter, Maxie Zeus

Foes: Batman, the Batman Family

POWERS AND ABILITIES

Expert in chemistry with a genius-level IQ; expert plotter and manipulator; many connections in the criminal underworld.

RUNNING MAN

After his latest scheme at Arkham was foiled by the intervention of the supernatural hero called the Spectre, Professor Milo tried to flee the country but was stopped by the Batman and his newest Batplane.

Often using his expertise to obtain positions of authority, Professor Milo is a talented chemist who has put his knowledge to evil ends many times. Most recently, Milo posed as a doctor at Arkham Asylum, sneaking patients into underground chambers for cult leader Deacon Blackfire. He was also a teacher at Gotham Academy until his corruption became apparent.

"...this man is suffering. He wants us to help him."

When allied with the cultist Deacon Blackfire, Milo used his knowledge of chemistry to drug Blackfire's recruits, forcing them to obey him.

HUMPTY DUMPTY

VITAL STATS

Real Name: Humphry Dumpler

Occupation: Criminal

Height: 6ft 3in

Weight: 349 lbs

Base: Gotham City

Ally: Great White Shark

Foes: Batman, Batgirl, the Batman Family

POWERS AND ABILITIES

Disturbed mind with a penchant for breaking things and trying to put them back together again; appears to have the intellect of a child; has a large body with substantial strength.

ALL FALL DOWN

Humpty Dumpty almost single-handedly changed the face of Gotham City by inadvertently destroying many of the large over-the-top props that formerly graced the town's famous skyline.

Humphry Dumpler's life fell apart after his home was destroyed by a misplaced wrecking ball. He soon became obsessed with taking things apart and putting them back again, including subway cars and traffic lights. Dubbed Humpty Dumpty, the unbalanced Dumpler caused an untold number of injuries due to the fact that he couldn't quite repair the damage he created.

"Snips and snails and puppy dog tails."

Often a resident at Arkham Asylum, Humpty Dumpty is not very popular—since he sometimes likes to "fix" people he views as broken.

HYPNOTIC

ROGUE

VITAL STATS

Real Name: Unknown
Occupation: Criminal
Height: 6ft
Weight: 197 lbs
Base: Gotham City
Allies: The Penguin,
Mr. Combustible, Mr.
Toxic, Imperceptible
Man, Mr. Mosaic,
Emperor Blackgate
Foes: Batman, the Batman
Family, the Falcone Family

POWERS AND ABILITIES

Highly intelligent; utilizes
radio control waves to
take over the minds of his
victims; maintains powerful
connections in the criminal
underworld.

THE EYES HAVE IT

Hypnotic saw himself facing
action in Gotham City sooner
than expected when he
battled Batman while aboard
the Penguin's Iceberg Casino.
He quickly discovered his
hypnotic abilities had no
effect on the Dark Knight.

Hypnotic made his debut in Gotham
City along with several other new
players who were organized and
mentored by the Penguin. As part of
his mentorship, Hypnotic was forced
to pay part of his earnings to the
Penguin. So when the Penguin's
empire was briefly taken over by
Emperor Blackgate, Hypnotic had no
qualms about switching allegiances.

Highly intelligent
crime boss

Uses radio
waves to
control minds

Shows little
loyalty to
anyone

*"Stand back. I'll take
control—"*

IMPERCEPTIBLE MAN

ROGUE

VITAL STATS

Real Name: Unknown
Occupation: Criminal
Height: Unknown
Weight: Unknown
Base: Gotham City
Allies: The Penguin, Mr. Toxic, Mr. Combustible, Hypnotic, Mr. Mosaic, Emperor Blackgate
Foes: Batman, the Batman Family, the Falcone Family

POWERS AND ABILITIES

Is completely invisible except for the clothing he chooses to wear; highly intelligent; many useful connections in the criminal underworld.

MARCHING ORDERS

Having previously worked for the Penguin, the Imperceptible Man and a few of his fellow criminals were called to a meeting by their temporary boss Ignatius Ogilvy, the future Emperor Blackgate.

The Imperceptible Man is a mysterious criminal whose powers remain a mystery to the majority of Gotham City's citizens. An employee of the Penguin, the Imperceptible Man's work was interrupted by a brief stint of cooperation with the Penguin's replacement, Emperor Blackgate, before he and his allies returned to work for the Penguin.

"What are we going to do?"

Always wears glasses

Natural leader and crime boss, despite being invisible

Clothes do not turn invisible like his skin

Wore gas mask during the Man-Bat epidemic

BIG TOP

VITAL STATS

Real Name: Unknown

Occupation: Criminal

Height: 5ft 9in

Weight: 567 lbs

Base: Gotham City

Allies: Professor Pyg, Mr. Toad, Le Cirque d'etrange

Foes: Dick Grayson, Robin, Batman

POWERS AND ABILITIES

Excess weight allows for nearly superhuman strength and endurance; excellent hand-to-hand combatant despite size; many connections in the criminal underworld.

THE BIG MYSTERY

So little is known about Big Top that there is some debate over whether the villain is male or female. Big Top insists upon wearing a tutu nearly all of the time, but has a fully-formed goatee.

Little is known about the super-villain Big Top. As a member of Le Cirque d'etrange, Big Top worked directly with Professor Pyg, and even stormed police headquarters to help fellow circus member, Mr. Toad, escape custody. Unfortunately for Big Top, Batman and Robin were on hand to bring the criminals to justice.

"Didn't Toad tell you he had friends?"

Weight lends to powerful strikes

Strange appearance intimidates foes

Is quicker than appears

LOCK-UP

VITAL STATS

Real Name: Lyle Bolton

Occupation: Criminal

Height: 6ft 2in

Weight: 240 lbs

Base: Gotham City

Allies: Cluemaster, Firefly, Signalman

Foes: Batman, the Batman Family, Spoiler

POWERS AND ABILITIES

Expert knowledge of police procedure; extremely fit and athletic; adept hand-to-hand combatant; known to use police weapons including baton; employs hi-tech weapons as well, including an electrified net.

IF YOU CAN'T BEAT 'EM...

In a renewed effort to eliminate the threat of Batman for good, Lock-Up teamed with several minor super-villains under the leadership of Cluemaster. Lock-Up and his allies were hoping that their meetings would remain under the radar due to their D-list status.

Lock-Up is really Lyle Bolton, a former security guard with a thirst for his own brand of justice. Having tried and failed to become a police officer, Lock-Up has no regard for the legal system. He began kidnapping super-villains and locking them up in makeshift prisons. After the Dark Knight stopped Lock-Up's crusade, Bolton became just another villain in Batman's Rogues Gallery.

Maintains private vendetta against injustice

Wears attire similar to police riot gear

Extremely athletic and muscular

"It's true what they say... it's brutal at the top."

KNIGHTFALL

VITAL STATS

Real Name: Charise Carnes
Occupation: Philanthropist, criminal
Height: 5ft 11in
Weight: 141 lbs
Base: Gotham City
Allies: Mirror, Grotesque, Gretel, James Gordon, Jr.
Foes: Batgirl, the Birds of Prey, Batwoman

POWERS AND ABILITIES

Expert manipulator and actor; extremely wealthy; adept martial artist with expertise in bladed weapons; severely mentally unhinged; many connections in high society and in the criminal underworld.

KNIGHTFALL DESCENDING
While the public saw Charise Carnes as a philanthropist trying to help the neighborhood of Cherry Hill, Batgirl discovered her cruelty early on. As Knightfall, Charise wanted to harm or kill every criminal in the city, no matter how minor his crime.

Raised by a wealthy real-estate baron, Charise Carnes was a teenager with a boyfriend named Trevor. But Charise was horrified when Trevor killed her family in front of her eyes. She didn't report her boyfriend, however, and was found guilty for his heinous acts. After a stint in Arkham Asylum, she reemerged as Knightfall, kidnapped Trevor, and made him pay for his crime.

The villain made a later bid for Gotham City, with many of Batgirl's old enemies. But with help from other female heroes, Batgirl's side prevailed.

"We're going to change Gotham forever."

VITAL STATS

Real Name: Phillipe Rianne

Occupation: Criminal

Height: 5ft 11in

Weight: 173 lbs

Base: Gotham City

Allies: Knightfall, Gretel, Mirror

Foes: The Birds of Prey, Batgirl

POWERS AND ABILITIES

Superhuman strength and endurance; mutation allows for the ability to absorb and release electricity.

LIGHTNING STRIKES

When he first battled Batgirl, Grotesque surprised her by absorbing and redirecting the electricity of a nearby lamp. When they battled for a second time, he threatened to use the electricity of a storm cloud, but was shot by a henchman with a change of heart.

Batgirl encountered the mysterious super-villain called Grotesque when he crashed a party for media mogul Theodore Aiklin, demanding that Aiklin hand over a valuable bottle of wine. Aiklin refused, Grotesque escaped, and Batgirl pursued him through the sewers. He later ambushed her, but was betrayed by one of his lackeys, and Batgirl took the villain down.

"What a lovely vintage she is."

Wears gargoyle-like mask

Mask once shattered by Batgirl

Channels electricity through club

Considers himself a cultured individual

Dresses in expensive clothing

GRETEL

VITAL STATS

Real Name: Lisly Bonner
Occupation: Criminal
Height: 5ft 10in
Weight: 140 lbs
Base: Gotham City
Allies: Knightfall,
Grotesque, Mirror
Foes: Batgirl, Batman,
the Birds of Prey

POWERS AND ABILITIES

Expert hand-to-hand
combatant; inability to feel
pain; able to control the
minds of men and make
them do her bidding;
proficient with firearms
and knives.

WORKING FOR CRUMBS
After failing to fulfill a contract to
murder Bruce Wayne due to the
intervention of Batgirl and Batman,
Gretel later continued her life of
crime working for Knightfall, another
powerful adversary of Batgirl.

An aspiring journalist hoping to be the
next Lois Lane, Lisly Bonner set her
sights on a criminal, Boss Whittaker.
When Whittaker found out she was
wearing a voice recorder, he shot Lisly,
and she plunged into the bay. The
incident unlocked her mind-control
powers, and she set out as the villain
Gretel, intent on gaining control over
the men that had made her powerless.

*"I envy that. I'm
green all over."*

Rendered bald from her injuries, Gretel now wears
different wigs to match her mood. She faced Batgirl
with green hair, and Batman wearing blue hair.

LORD DEATH MAN

VITAL STATS

Real Name: Unknown
Occupation: Criminal
Height: 5ft 11in
Weight: 168 lbs
Base: Mobile
Allies: Leviathan, variety of henchmen
Foes: Rā's al Ghūl, Batman Japan, Batman, Dr. Darrk, Talon, the Outsiders

POWERS AND ABILITIES

Able to die and come back to life; mentally unstable; superhuman durability and endurance; capable hand-to-hand combatant; utterly fearless due to his particular condition.

SKELETONS IN THE CLOSET

After the fall of Leviathan, Rā's al Ghūl captured Lord Death Man in the hope of using the villain's death powers to his advantage. When Talon broke into one of al Ghūl's hideouts, he was forced to contend with the skeletal criminal.

A former opponent of Batman's, Lord Death Man reemerged recently in Japan when he killed the original Mr. Unknown. On a Batman, Inc. mission, Batman and Catwoman stopped Lord Death Man with the help of Jiro Osamu, Mr. Unknown's successor and the future Batman Japan. Unable to die, Lord Death Man has become a repeated thorn in Batman's side.

"Welcome to the Dead Heroes Club!"

Lord Death Man rarely takes life-and-death situations seriously, despite having clashed with Talon, the Outsiders, and even Batman and Robin in the past.

MARIONETTE

VITAL STATS

Real Name: Unknown, called "Mali"

Occupation: Criminal

Height: 5ft 9in

Weight: 147 lbs

Base: Chicago

Ally: Dick Grayson

Foes: Johnny Spade, the Mad Hatter

POWERS AND ABILITIES

Ability to mimic the movement and fighting techniques of others after witnessing them in action; extremely fit, fast, and agile; excellent hand-to-hand combatant.

UNLIKELY ALLIES

Marionette is the Catwoman to Nightwing's Batman. Appearing to have a similar moral code, the two have worked together in the past. However, they still remain on opposite sides of the law.

The Mad Hatter's manipulation altered her mind

Unbalanced mind requires Kanium to function

Skintight suit allows her range of movement

Often steals to acquire Kanium

The young Mali was once one of the Mad Hatter's favorite obsessions. Kidnapped into doing his mind-controlled bidding as his "Alice," she was shot by the Hatter. Cursed with a condition called "personality slipping," Mali relies on a rare drug, Kanium, to balance her mind. She does whatever she needs to, as Marionette, to keep a constant supply of the medicine.

*"This **one wants to pull our strings.**"*

TWEEDLEDEE AND TWEEDLEDUM

ROGUE

VITAL STATS

Real Names: Deever and Dumfree Tweed

Occupation: Criminals

Height: Both 5ft 7in

Weight: Both 187 lbs

Base: Gotham City

Ally: The Mad Hatter

Foes: Batman, the Batman Family

POWERS AND ABILITIES

Capable hand-to-hand combatants; very intelligent; proficient in a variety of weapons.

DUMB AND DUMBER

More often than not, Tweedledee and Tweedledum serve as the insane villain Mad Hatter's hired muscle. Recently, they helped the Mad Hatter ransack homeless shelters in a frenzied search for the Hatter's delusional obsession, his lost "Alice."

The Mad Hatter is not the only villain to take his name from Lewis Carroll's book, *Through the Looking Glass*. When look-alike cousins, Deever and Dumfree Tweed, embarked on a life of crime, they adopted the identities of Tweedledee and Tweedledum. Having menaced Batman on their own, they have become allied with the Hatter.

"Don't worry boss. We gonna—"
"—crush the little man."

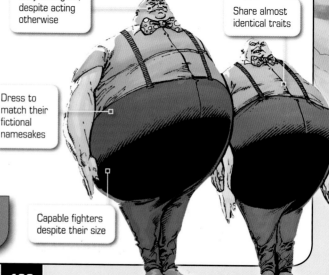

Very intelligent, despite acting otherwise

Share almost identical traits

Dress to match their fictional namesakes

Capable fighters despite their size

HERETIC

VITAL STATS

Real Name: None
Occupation: Terrorist
Height: 7ft 4in
Weight: 345 lbs
Base: Mobile
Allies: Talia al Ghūl,
Leviathan
Foes: Batman, Robin,
the Batman Family

POWERS AND ABILITIES

Superhuman strength,
endurance, and durability;
weapons expert; master
swordsman; excellent
hand-to-hand combatant;
seemingly unaffected by
pain; wears protective
armor that includes a
jetpack to enable flight.

BORN TO KILL

The Heretic was meant
to be Robin's replacement,
one Talia made sure
Damian was aware of
before she cast him out
of her family. The Heretic
trained in Yemen and
killed many superhumans
in preparation for his role
as Talia's ally.

Grown in a lab and hatched out of
a whale carcass by Talia al Ghūl and
her clandestine Leviathan organization,
the Heretic was a grotesquely aged
"brother" to Talia's son, Damian
Wayne—also known as Robin.
Desperate to prove his love to Talia,
the Heretic served her, destroying
anyone who threatened Leviathan,
including, eventually, Damian himself.

*"I watch. I listen. I learn.
I am Batman now."*

Underneath his robes, the Heretic wore
Batman-styled armor. Despite his desire
to please his mother, Talia hated the Heretic.

LADY VIC

ROGUE

VITAL STATS

Real Name: Lady Elaine Marsh-Morton

Occupation: Assassin

Height: 5ft 6in

Weight: 120 lbs

Base: England

Ally: Charlie Caligula

Foes: Batwing, Nightwing

POWERS AND ABILITIES

Expert assassin, martial artist, hand-to-hand combatant, and sharp-shooter; prefers to use weapons that are old family heirlooms; well connected in the criminal underworld; quick, fit, agile, and cunning.

LADY OF THE WORLD
Lady Vic seems at home in any environment, from the bright daytime streets of Mumbai, India, to the dark shadows of the Gotham City night. She is a professional, and usually does her job quickly and efficiently.

Lady Vic's name is short for "Lady Victim," but her actions point to her being more the predator than the prey. Hailing from a long line of British mercenaries, Lady Vic takes her job seriously. Recently, she nearly killed Batwing after taking on a mission to destroy any and all bat-themed vigilantes she encountered during her stay in Gotham City.

"You're not the hero. You're a paycheck."

When Lady Vic first met Batwing, she easily bested the hero, despite his armored suit of advanced technology.

MERRYMAKER

ROGUE

VITAL STATS

Real Name: Dr. Byron Merideth

Occupation: Criminal, former psychiatrist

Height: 6ft 1in

Weight: 194 lbs

Base: Gotham City

Allies: Harley Quinn, Mr. Freeze, Professor Pyg, Scarecrow

Foes: Batman, the Batman Family

POWERS AND ABILITIES

Behavioral modification expert, willing to utilize extreme and controversial methods; master manipulator; highly intelligent; access to Arkham Asylum patients.

IN LEAGUE WITH A MADMAN

The Merrymaker founded the League of Smiles, a gang devoted to the Joker. While he had no connection to the Clown Prince of Crime himself, he was more than willing to use the Joker's reputation for his own selfish gain.

A psychiatrist at Arkham Asylum, Dr. Byron Merideth was one of the doctors assigned to evaluate the Joker. He then started up a private psychiatric practice to exploit those influenced by the Joker. Adopting the persona of the masked Merrymaker, he convinced his Joker-obsessed patients to do his bidding as soldiers for the Joker's "grand crusade."

"Merrymaker and the League of Smiles are just getting started."

The Merrymaker aided Scarecrow and a few other Arkham inmates in creating a mass hallucination in Gotham City known as Gothtopia.

MR. TOXIC

ROGUE

VITAL STATS

Real Name: Hugh Marder
Occupation: Scientist,
criminal
Height: 6ft 4in
Weight: 240 lbs
Base: Gotham City
Allies: The Penguin,
Mr. Combustible,
Imperceptible Man,
Professor Radium
Foes: Batman, the
Batman Family

POWERS AND ABILITIES

Energy projection; excellent
hand-to-hand combatant;
genius-level intellect despite
being mentally unbalanced;
connections to Gotham
City's criminal underworld.

TOXIC TOUCH

Batman once battled Mr. Toxic in a
laboratory inside Wayne Tower. The
only way he could overcome Toxic's
energy projections was by using a
prototype energy deflector from his
Utility Belt, developed by Lucius Fox.

Working on a way to travel forward
in time, scientist Hugh Marder
ran into problems. Wanting to
cure his own genetic disease,
Marder began creating clones of
himself that eventually deteriorated.
Unable to stop his disease, Marder
adopted the protective suit of
Professor Radium while his most
stable clone became Mr. Toxic.

*"I am no longer a carbon copy of
you! I am your equal now, Marder!"*

Mind unbalanced
after faulty
experiment

Projects
crackling energy

Helmet has been
shattered by
Batman

VORTEX

VITAL STATS

Real Name: Unknown

Occupation: Criminal, former quantum physicist

Height: 6ft

Weight: 203 lbs

Base: Gotham City

Allies: Catwoman, Cheetah, Hellhound

Foes: Batman, the Batman Family, Killer Frost

POWERS AND ABILITIES

Force-based powers allow him to repel anything near his person; athletic build; need for revenge against his enemies.

BARS AND STRIPES

Vortex met Catwoman inside Arkham Asylum. To escape her cell, she convinced Vortex to stop taking his medicine and therefore activate his powers.

Vortex started out as a quantum physicist, working on an atom smasher. When he was sucked into the vortex of his own creation, he gained fantastic powers but lost some of his sanity. "Zebra man" found camaraderie among the criminal sect, and recently teamed up with Cheetah and several other animal-themed criminals including another Gotham City villain, Hellhound.

"Now I'm awake and I got some scores to settle."

Mentally unbalanced after accident

Force stripes cover entire body

Wears minimalistic costume

Powers can be held in check by medicine

MR. COMBUSTIBLE

ROGUE

VITAL STATS

Real Name: Unknown
Occupation: Criminal
Height: 6ft 3in
Weight: 199 lbs
Base: Gotham City
Allies: The Penguin, Mr. Toxic, Imperceptible Man, Hypnotic, Mr. Mosaic
Foes: Batman, the Batman Family, the Falcone Family

POWERS AND ABILITIES

Seemingly made up of a mysterious chemical formula; can sense chemical compounds like explosives; very intelligent leader; many connections in the criminal underworld.

A SHINING JEWEL

Mr. Combustible is highly resourceful and organized. This helped him rob several jewelry stores for Emperor Blackgate when a Man-Bat virus spread throughout Gotham City thanks to Blackgate's plotting.

While Mr. Combustible's past remains a mystery, he seems a perfect fit as a Gotham City crime lord, with his strange looks and aristocratic personality. Forced to work for the Penguin when he arrived in the city, Mr. Combustible has made the most of his situation by staying loyal to him, even during the brief time Emperor Blackgate took control of the Penguin's criminal empire.

"I'm sensing the presence of high explosives in this chamber!"

During a recent battle between Arkham Asylum inmates and Blackgate prisoners, Mr. Combustible had his head shattered, but survived the encounter.

VENTRILOQUIST

ROGUE

VITAL STATS

Real Name: Shauna Belzer
Occupation: Criminal
Height: 5ft 11in
Weight: 115 lbs
Base: Gotham City
Allies: "Ferdie,"
the Secret Six
Foes: Batman, Batgirl,
the Riddler

POWERS AND ABILITIES

Uses telekinetic abilities
to control the bodies
of others; connections
in the criminal
underworld; has a
dangerously disturbed
mind; manipulates
puppet to use as a
terrifying weapon.

SHARP AS A SPLINTER

Shauna customized a puppet
she stole from a childhood
entertainer, placing drills
in his palms and treating
"Ferdie" as if he were alive.
She often uses Ferdie to
attack her victims.

Appears
sickly
and frail

Shauna Belzer was born with a twin
brother who stole the limelight. While
Shauna was dubbed "Shabby Shauna"
by schoolmates, her brother became
a child star. Discovering she had
telekinetic abilities, she used them to
punish her teasing classmates, and her
twin brother. As an adult, she began
a criminal career as the Ventriloquist,
naming her puppet after her brother.

Telekinetic ability
makes her a top
ventriloquist

Her puppet
brings out
her dark side

*"I don't like it when people
are rude, Ferdie."*

WRATH

ROGUE

VITAL STATS

Real Name: E.D. Caldwell

Occupation: CEO of Caldwell Technologies, criminal

Height: 6ft 2in

Weight: 210 lbs

Base: Gotham City

Allies: Emperor Blackgate, Scorn

Foes: Batman, Alfred Pennyworth, G.C.P.D.

POWERS AND ABILITIES

Extremely intelligent; a wealthy businessman; access to cutting-edge weapons and vehicles; armored suit equipped with variety of weapons; expert martial artist and hand-to-hand combatant.

DYSFUNCTIONAL DUO

Like Batman, Wrath considers himself a loner. But just as the Batman had adopted partners in the form of Robin and Batgirl, Wrath hired a cop killer in the form of Scorn. But when Scorn failed a mission, Wrath simply killed him.

The son of Mallory Caldwell, a man killed by the G.C.P.D., E.D. Caldwell went on to found Caldwell Technologies, a weapons manufacturer. Wanting vengeance for his father's death, he made a bid to purchase Wayne Enterprises, but Bruce Wayne rejected his offer. Caldwell nonetheless launched an assault on the G.C.P.D., stopped only by Batman's interference.

"...this is a game you're certain to lose."

Lenses enhance his vision

Highly armored suit

Shock gloves can dispense 60,000 watts of current

VELVET TIGER

ROGUE

VITAL STATS

Real Name: Lani Gilbert

Occupation: Criminal, CEO of GilCom

Height: 5ft 5in

Weight: 112 lbs

Base: Mobile

Allies: Stolen tigers

Foes: Batgirl, Batwing

POWERS AND ABILITIES

Extremely fast and agile; has razor-sharp claws capable of cutting through cords easily; adept hand-to-hand combatant; computer expert; skilled in the use of knives.

EARNING HER STRIPES

When Batgirl first faced Velvet Tiger, she was taken by surprise by the villain's prowess in a fight. Velvet Tiger turned the tables on Batgirl, injecting the Super Hero with her own tranquilizer dart.

When a tiger attacked the office building of Luke Fox's new startup, FoxTek, Batgirl got involved, fighting off a second tiger attack at a similar company. Batgirl discovered this was the handiwork of a new villain in Gotham City, Velvet Tiger. Realizing that this villain was Lani Gilbert, CEO of the failing tech company GilCom, Batgirl trailed Velvet Tiger, defeating her with the help of a remote-guided Batcycle.

"Better to live one year as a tiger, than a hundred as a sheep."

Velvet Tiger picked the wrong fight by kidnapping Jo, a friend of Batgirl's. Batgirl fought hard to defeat the villain's tigers, allowing Jo to escape.

MORTICIAN

VITAL STATS

Real Name: Porter Vito
Occupation: Criminal
Height: 6ft
Weight: 176 lbs
Base: Gotham City
Allies: The dead
Foes: Batman, the Batman Family

POWERS AND ABILITIES

Brilliant chemist; developed a formula to bring dead bodies to life; obsessed with stopping death.

WAKE THE DEAD

The Mortician was one of the many Batman villains who escaped Arkham Asylum during a recent breakout. He's not one to shy away from a good riot, and still holds a grudge against the Caped Crusader.

After the death of his parents, the Mortician became obsessed with bringing the dead back to life. A gifted chemist who had been criticized by his parents for indulging in the sciences, he battled Batman after one of the "zombies" he created committed murder. After Batman defeated the Mortician's army of the undead, the villain used a serum to put his parents to rest once more.

"I often dream of killing him."

The Mortician was one of the inmates Maggie Sawyer and Batwoman interviewed when Batwoman was trying to defeat the Dark Knight.

TUSK

VITAL STATS

Real Name: Unknown

Occupation: Gang boss

Height: 8ft 2in

Weight: 1,575 lbs

Base: Gotham City

Allies: His criminal lackeys

Foes: Dick Grayson, Batman, Robin

POWERS AND ABILITIES

Superhuman strength and endurance; extremely tough skin that allows for enhanced durability; gang leader with many connections in the Gotham City underworld.

DE-TUSKED

While Tusk gained the upper hand against Batman on their first encounter, the villain ultimately lost the fight thanks to Robin, who broke off one of the criminal's tusks. Later, Damian Wayne broke off the other tusk.

Little is known about Tusk's origins. Batman began to concentrate on the massive gangster's activities years ago, when Dick Grayson was out on his first official night of patrol as Robin. Although Batman fired Robin for not listening to his orders, Robin attacked Tusk, and managed to knock the villain from a helicopter, earning his place by Batman's side.

"Time to pick on somebody my size."

Why Tusk resembles an elephant remains a mystery, but what is known is that he has repeatedly returned to plague Dick Grayson.

NOBODY

VITAL STATS

Real Name: Morgan Ducard
Occupation: Mercenary
Height: 6ft 1in
Weight: 214 lbs
Base: Gotham City
Allies: Henri Ducard, NoBody II
Foes: Batman, Batman, Inc., Robin

POWERS AND ABILITIES

Highly trained martial artist and assassin; hi-tech weaponized armored suit offers invisibility cloaking; enhanced vision; palm energy blasts; daughter currently wears similar suit with sonic upgrades.

GHOST FROM THE PAST

Batman first became aware of NoBody's campaign against him when the villain killed the Batman, Inc. agent known as the Batman of Moscow. NoBody's desire for revenge was strong—he blamed Batman for disgracing him in front of his father.

Daughter wears similar suit after Morgan's death

Special investigator Henri Ducard trained his son Morgan in the ways of manhunting alongside Bruce Wayne —fostering a rivalry between Morgan and Bruce. Bruce later quit his training, and defeated Morgan as he tried to leave. Morgan returned as the villain NoBody, but was killed by Robin. His daughter, Maya Ducard, took on the role of NoBody.

Hi-tech invisibility capabilities

Armored suit protects from damage

> *"...You know I'll be back to kill you all..."*

TIGER SHARK

ROGUE

VITAL STATS

Real Name: Unknown
Occupation: Criminal
Height: 6ft 1in
Weight: 203 lbs
Base: Gotham City
Allies: Carmine Falcone, Bone
Foes: Dick Grayson, Batman, the Batman Family

POWERS AND ABILITIES

Adept hand-to-hand combatant; excellent leader; has many ties in the criminal underworld; drawn to endangered animals; uses a cane as a weapon as well as firearms.

THE FOOD CHAIN

When Carmine Falcone returned to Gotham City for a short period, Tiger Shark began working as his enforcer. Despite having an employer, Tiger Shark maintained a loyal entourage of lackeys who constantly spoke on his behalf.

A modern day pirate and smuggler, Tiger Shark made a major play to do business in Gotham City during the brief period when Dick Grayson took over for Bruce Wayne as Batman. Normally keeping just far enough off the coast of Gotham City to remain outside Coast Guard jurisdiction, Tiger Shark once used a gas pipeline to move material in and out of the city.

"The tides will reclaim us."

Mask made of seal skin

Hieroglyphics tattooed on tongue

Prefers clothing made from endangered species

NOCTURNA

VITAL STATS

Real Name: Natalia Mitternacht

Occupation: Criminal

Height: 5ft 10in

Weight: 140 lbs

Base: Gotham City

Allies: Night-Thief, Wolf Spider, Morgaine le Fey

Foes: Batwoman, Maggie Sawyer, Batman, Killshot, the Unknowns

POWERS AND ABILITIES

Able to hypnotize others into believing a false reality or to be instantly smitten by her charms; connections to high society and the criminal world; adept at mind games.

WICKED WITCH

Nocturna once fought Batwoman when the evil sorceress Morgaine le Fey altered reality to appear like something out of a fantasy novel. Nocturna worked directly for le Fey until the Unknowns restored the world to its natural state.

A former foe of Batman's, Nocturna first crossed Batwoman's path when a villain named Wolf Spider broke her out of Arkham Asylum. She later used her hypnotic skills to be legally freed from the institution. Meeting Kate Kane (Batwoman) soon after, Nocturna came close to becoming a hero—until Batwoman discovered her crooked ways and defeated her.

Capable hand-to-hand combatant

Very intelligent and a master planner

Skilled fighter who keeps in shape

"Hello, Batwoman. Lovely to see you again."

TERMINUS

VITAL STATS

Real Name: Unknown
Occupation: Criminal
Height: 6ft 4in
Weight: 240 lbs
Base: Gotham City
Allies: Scallop, Bootface, Smush, Bathead
Foes: Batman, the Batman Family

POWERS AND ABILITIES

Employs a group of loyal lackeys who do his dirty work; vast stream of revenue enables purchase of warheads and technology to preserve his own life; armored battle suit provides enhanced strength and endurance.

TERMINAL CASE

Terminus's rapidly deteriorating body required constant injections to sustain his life. He adopted a massive battle suit to fight Batman before his own death.

Terminus's origins are mysterious. A villain whose body was literally falling apart, he knew the exact time of his upcoming death. Blaming Batman for his situation, he hired a team of criminals that had each been scarred by earlier encounters with Batman. They attacked Gotham City's citizens before Terminus unleashed a warhead —which was quickly defused by Batman.

Battle suit armed with hi-tech weaponry

Body deteriorating at rapid pace

Technology helps to maintain life

"...I wanted to see you die inside a little, right before I do."

PROFESSOR PYG

VITAL STATS

Real Name: Lazlo Valentin
Occupation: Criminal
Height: 5ft 11in
Weight: 264 lbs
Base: Gotham City
Allies: Dr. Hurt,
Le Cirque d'etrange
Foes: Batman, Dick Grayson,
Robin, Carmine Falcone

POWERS AND ABILITIES

Manic, unpredictable
behavior; often aided by
henchmen and an army
of mind-altered Dollotrons;
capable hand-to-hand
combatant; considers
murder and violence
an art form.

THIS LITTLE PIGGY WENT TO GOTHAM CITY

After his laboratory,
located at Sinclair's
Meats in Old Gotham,
was burned down,
Professor Pyg sought
vengeance. He
retaliated against
his attacker, Carmine
Falcone, deciding
that all of Gotham
City would now
serve as his lab.

Recently
employed animal-
masked lackeys

Wears pig mask
at all times

When Batman first encountered the
villain calling himself Professor Pyg, it
wasn't Bruce Wayne wearing the cape
and cowl, it was Dick Grayson. In his
brief stint as Batman, Grayson teamed
with Robin to take down Pyg, a former
low rent circus boss who decided to
become an underworld criminal.
The disturbed Pyg ran his operations
from a deserted amusement park.

*"Pyg will make
you perfect."*

KGBEAST

ROGUE

VITAL STATS

Real Name: Anatoli Knyazev

Occupation: Mercenary

Height: 6ft 3in

Weight: 231 lbs

Base: Russia

Allies: NKVDemon, Cheshire, Mayhem

Foes: Batman, Aquaman, the Others

POWERS AND ABILITIES

Expert assassin, hand-to-hand combatant, and acrobat; superhuman strength, endurance, and durability; adept spy with strong connections in the intelligence and criminal worlds; weapons expert; fully stocked Utility Belt.

MAKING MAYHEM

As a member of an organization called Mayhem, KGBeast teamed with several other heavyweight mercenaries, including his apprentice, the NKVDemon. Their plot to take over the world was foiled by the Others.

An expert assassin, KGBeast came to Gotham City years ago and clashed with Batman. Choosing to lose his own hand rather than admit defeat to the Dark Knight, KGBeast nevertheless ultimately failed in his mission. He continues to fight for Russia's "old ways," and recently fought with Aquaman and his team of allies called the Others.

"We shall restore our country to what it once was..."

Wears mask to hide his scarred face

Protective suit bears colors of the Soviet Union

Turned his severed hand into a weapon

RATCATCHER

VITAL STATS

Real Name: Otis Flannegan

Occupation: Criminal

Height: 5ft 10in

Weight: 160 lbs

Base: Gotham City

Allies: Cluemaster, Menace, Firefly, Signalman, Lock-Up

Foes: Batman, Batwing, the Batman Family

POWERS AND ABILITIES

Communicates with and controls rats; has connections to Gotham City's underground community and several above-ground criminals as well.

RAT FINK

Severely mentally unbalanced, the Ratcatcher keeps a live rat in his helmet. He often has conversations with his rodents, and uses them to spy on people on Gotham City's streets, essentially giving him eyes and ears everywhere.

A citizen of the underground, the vast network of cities and towns below Gotham City, the Ratcatcher is obsessed with other residents of that dark world: rats. Working with the villain Menace, he used his command over rodents to help kidnap Batwing's sister, Tiffany Fox. He later joined forces with Cluemaster in an attempt to destroy Batman for good.

"Heigh-ho the derry-o the cheese goes insane!"

The Ratcatcher has trouble speaking. He prefers to communicate with his rodent allies rather than the crime bosses he's worked with.

SUMO

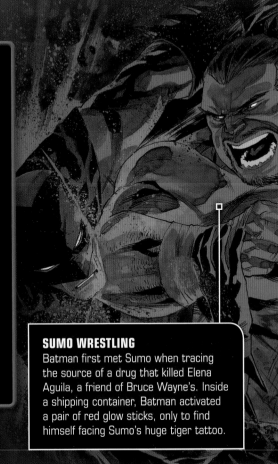

VITAL STATS

Real Name: Unknown
Occupation: Criminal
Height: 6ft 5in
Weight: 607 lbs
Base: Gotham City
Allies: The Squid,
Arkham Asylum inmates
Foes: Batman, Resurrection
Man, Bane

POWERS AND ABILITIES

Extremely strong and
heavy; quicker than his
appearance implies; many
connections in the criminal
underworld; maintains
impressive endurance
and durability.

SUMO WRESTLING

Batman first met Sumo when tracing
the source of a drug that killed Elena
Aguila, a friend of Bruce Wayne's. Inside
a shipping container, Batman activated
a pair of red glow sticks, only to find
himself facing Sumo's huge tiger tattoo.

A familiar face behind the bars
at Arkham Asylum, Sumo cuts an
intimidating figure in the criminal
underworld. Batman first encountered
the villain when he interrupted a
smuggling ring Sumo had been running
at Gotham City's docks. Batman
triumphed over the enormous villain,
learning that Sumo had worked with
a Gotham City crime boss, the Squid.

Mentally
unstable, he
enjoys violence

Wears scant
clothing and a
sumo's mawashi

Enormous body
can crush
opponents

*"I thought bats could
see in the dark!"*

RED ALICE

NEUTRAL

VITAL STATS

Real Name: Elizabeth Kane

Occupation: Vigilante, former criminal

Height: 5ft 11in

Weight: 141 lbs

Base: Mobile

Allies: Batwoman, the Unknowns

Foes: Mr. Bones, Morgaine le Fey, Nocturna

POWERS AND ABILITIES

Skilled martial artist and gymnast; extensive understanding of military procedure; damaged mind from past trauma; adept hand-to-hand combatant; excellent marksman; wears protective suit equipped with variety of gadgets.

ALICE DOESN'T LIVE HERE ANYMORE

Red Alice and Batwoman are sisters, but they couldn't be more different. Red Alice is constantly struggling with her sanity, often quoting lines from Lewis Carroll's *Through the Looking Glass* as her own speech.

As a young girl, Beth Kane was kidnapped alongside her twin sister, Kate Kane, and their mother. While their father, Jacob Kane, managed to rescue Kate, Beth was presumed dead, only to reemerge as the very disturbed super-villain Red Alice. Fighting her own sister who had adopted the identity of Batwoman, Red Alice was eventually defeated by her Super Hero twin.

"Don't worry. I'm not here to kill you."

After surviving her battle with Batwoman, Red Alice straightened out her life to become a vigilante on the right side of the law.

THE SQUID

VITAL STATS

Real Name: Lawrence Loman

Occupation: Criminal

Height: 5ft 6in

Weight: 173 lbs

Base: Gotham City

Allies: Sumo, Calendar Man

Foes: Batman, Harvey Bullock

POWERS AND ABILITIES

Intelligent strategist and leader; many connections in the criminal underworld.

TANKED

The Squid had no qualms about making an example out of someone who had wronged him. When his own brother's crew stole from him, the Squid dropped one of the men into the tank of a deadly giant squid.

The Squid was a Gotham City crime boss who attracted Batman's attention after the death of Bruce Wayne's friend, Elena Aguila. Looking into Elena's death, Batman uncovered a network of criminals that included the Squid. Tracking him to an abandoned aquarium, Batman overcame the villain's pet squid before the Squid was killed by a rival criminal.

Comfortable, lightweight jacket

No costume needed to exude an air of danger

Not afraid to get his own hands dirty

"...Gotham City is the monster that needs to be fed."

INDEX

Main entries are in **bold**.

ARTIST ACKNOWLEDGMENTS

Christian Alamy, Juan Albarran, Oclair Albert, Rafael Albuquerque, Laura Alfred, Michael Alfred, Marlo Alquiza, Brad Anderson, Marc Andreyko, Joy Ang, Ulises Arreola, Mahmud Asrar, Michael Atiyeh, Tony Aviña, Matt Banning, Al Barrionuevo, Eddy Barrows, Jacob Bear, David Beaty, Tony Bedard, Ed Benes, Mariah Benes, Bengal, Ryan Benjamin, Marguerite Bennet, Joe Bennett, Rain Beredo, Lee Bermejo, W. Haden Blackman, Fernando Blanco, Blond, Roger Bonet, James Bonny, Brett Booth, Geraldo Borges, Andrei Bressan, Vera Brosgol, Jimmy Broxton, Brian Buccellato, Cullen Bunn, Riccardo Burchielli, Chris Burnham, Jim Calafiore, Greg Capullo, Juan Castro, Keith Champagne, Howard Chaykin, Clio Chiang, ChrisCross, June Chung, Vicente Cifuentes, Scott Clark, Andy Clarke, Ronan Cliquet, Becky Cloonan, Andre Coelho, David Cole, Simon Coleby, Amanda Conner, Will Conrad, Darwyn Cooke, Paul Cornell, Jorge Corona, Jeromy Cox, Wes Craig, Andrew Dalhouse, Federico Dallacchio, Tony S. Daniel, Marc Deering, Tom DeFalco, Werther Dell'Edera, Jesse Delperdang, Tom Derenick, Johnny Desjardins, Dan DiDio, Andy Diggle, Rachel Dodson, Terry Dodson, Jed Dougherty, Christian Duce, Dale Eaglesham, Scott Eaton, Gabe Eltaeb, Nathan Eyring, Jason Fabok, Nathan Fairbairn, Romulo Fajardo, Jr., Ray Fawkes, Raul Fernandez, Eber Ferreira, Julio Ferreira, Juan Ferreyra, Pascal Ferry, David Finch, Meredith Finch, Brenden Fletcher, Sandu Florea, Fabrizio Florentino, Jorge Fornes, Gary Frank, Derek Fridolfs, Richard Friend, Lee Garbett, Alex Garner, Javier Garrón, Sterling Gates, Dave Geraci, Drew Geraci, Ransom Getty, Sunny Gho, Keith Giffen, Jonathan Glapion, Adam Glass, Patrick Gleeson, Joel Gomez, Julius Gopez, Mick Gray, Justin Gray, Dan Green, Michael Green, Ig Guara, R.M. Guera, Andres Guinaldo, Scott Hanna, Chad Hardin, Joe Harris, James Harvey, Jeremy Haun, Rob Haynes, Doug Hazlewood, Daniel Henriques, Scott Hepburn, Meghan Hetrick, Hi-Fi Design, Kyle Higgins, David Hine, Bryan Hitch, Sandra Hope, Corin Howell, Adam Hughes, Ken Hunt, Rob Hunter, Gregg Hurwitz, Frazer Irving, Mark Irwin, Jack Jadson, Al Jaffee, Mikel Janín, Georges Jeanty, Paul Jenkins, Jorge Jimenez, Jock, Geoff Johns, Staz Johnson, Mike Johnson, Henrik Jonsson, Ruy José, Juancho, Dan Jurgens, John Kalisz, Jon Katz, Karl Kerschi, Karl Kesel, Tom King, Tyler Kirkham, Scott Kolins, Ales Kot, Andrew Kreisberg, Andy Kubert, Szymon Kudranski, Michel Lacombe, José Ladrönn, David Lafuente, Serge Lapointe, Ken Lashley, John Layman, Jae Lee, Jim Lee, Jay Leisten, Jeff Lemire, Rick Leonardi, Yishan Li, Rob Liefeld, LLC, Scott Lobdell, Jeph Loeb, Alvaro Lopez, David Lopez, Emilio Lopez, Aaron Lopresti, Lee Loughridge, Jorge Lucas, Ant Lucia, Emanuela Lupacchino, Doug Mahnke, Marcelo Maiolo, Guy Major, Alex Maleev, Francis Manapul, Leandro Manco, Clay Mann, Guillem March, Alitha Martinez, Allen Martinez, Alvaro Martinez, Stefano Martino, Christy Marx, José Marzan, Jr., Jason Masters, J.P. Mayer, Dave McCaig, Ray McCarthy, Trevor McCarthy, Scott McDaniel, Mike McKone, Lan Medina, Hermann Mejia, Javier Mena, Jaime Mendoza, Jesús Merino, Jonboy Meyers, Danny Miki, Romano Molenaar, Jorge Molina, Sula Moon, Stephen Mooney, Tomeu Morey, Moritat, Grant Morrison, Paul Mounts, Dustin Nguyen, Tom Nguyen, Fabian Nicieza, Ann Nocenti, Mike Norton, Kevin Nowlan, Sonia Oback, Patrick Olliffe, Guillermo Ortego, Andy Owens, Agustin Padilla, Greg Pak, Jimmy Palmiotti, Dan Panosian, Eduardo Pansica, Pete Pantazis, Yanick Paquette, Jeff Parker, Sean Parsons, Fernando Pasarin, Allen Passalaqua, Jason Pearson, Paul Pelletier, Pere Perez, Cris Peter, Will Pfeifer, Javier Piña, FCO Plascencia, Francis Portela, Howard Porter, Eric Powell, Joe Prado, Jack Purcell, Joe Quinones, Wil Quintana, Frank Quitely, Khary Randolph, Norm Rapmund, John Rauch, Sal Regla, Ivan Reis, Rod Reis, Cliff Richards, Tom Richmond, Jeremy Roberts, Roger Robinson, Kenneth Rocafort, Robson Rocha, Prentis Rollins, Alex Ross, Stéphane Roux, Felix Ruiz, Matt Ryan, Sean Ryan, Juan Jose Ryp, Jesús Saíz, Edgar Salazar, Tim Sale, Daniel Sampere, Rafa Sandoval, Derlis Santacruz, Trevor Scott, Tim Seeley, Emanuel Simeoni, Gail Simone, Alex Sinclair, Paulo Siqueira, Dan Slott, Brett Smith, Scott Snyder, Ben Sokolowski, Ryan Sook, Andrea Sorrentino, Chris Sotomayor, Peter Steigerwald, Cameron Stewart, Jeff Stokely, RC Stoodios, Karl Story, Carrie Strachan, Mico Suayan, Goran Sudzuka, Duane Swierczynski, Ardian Syaf, Phillip Tan, Babs Tarr, Jordi Tarragona, Ben Templesmith, Art Thibert, Frank Tieri, Marcus To, Peter Tomasi, Andy Troy, James Tynion IV, Ethan Van Sciver, Roberto Viacava, Dexter Vines, Alessandro Vitti, Joe Weems, Scott Williams, J.H. Williams III, Judd Winick, Ryan Winn, Marv Wolfman, Walden Wong, Jason Wright, Annie Wu, Matt Yackey, Craig Young, Richard Zajac, Patrick Zircher

SENIOR EDITOR Victoria Taylor
PROJECT EDITOR Shari Last
EDITOR Laura Nickoll
SENIOR DESIGNER Robert Perry
DESIGNERS Chris Gould, Pallavi Kapur
DTP DESIGNERS Umesh Singh Rawat, Rajdeep Singh
PRE-PRODUCTION PRODUCER Siu Yin Chan
PRE-PRODUCTION MANAGER Sunil Sharma
SENIOR PRODUCER Alex Bell
MANAGING EDITOR Sadie Smith
MANAGING ART EDITORS Ron Stobbart, Neha Ahuja
PUBLISHER Julie Ferris
ART DIRECTOR Lisa Lanzarini
PUBLISHING DIRECTOR Simon Beecroft

ADDITIONAL DESIGN Dynamo Limited

Dorling Kindersley would like to thank Josh Anderson and Amy Weingartner at Warner Bros. Global Publishing and Leah Tuttle at DC Entertainment. Thanks also to Julia March for the index, Joel Kempson, Lauren Nesworthy, Lisa Stock, and Chitra Subramanyam for editorial assistance, and Lisa Robb, Radhika Banerjee, and Ishita Chawla for design assistance.

First American Edition, 2016
Published in the United States by DK Publishing
345 Hudson Street, New York, New York 10014

Page design Copyright © 2016 Dorling Kindersley Limited
DK, a Division of Penguin Random House LLC
16 17 18 19 10 9 8 7 6 5 4 3 2 1
001-264931-Feb/16

A WORLD OF IDEAS:
SEE ALL THERE IS TO KNOW
www.dk.com
www.dccomics.com